Open Forum

ACADEMIC LISTENING AND SPEAKING

1

OXFORD
UNIVERSITY PRESS

OXFORD
UNIVERSITY PRESS

198 Madison Avenue
New York, NY 10016 USA

Great Clarendon Street, Oxford ox2 6dp UK

Oxford University Press is a department of the University of Oxford.
It furthers the University's objective of excellence in research, scholarship,
and education by publishing worldwide in

Oxford New York

Auckland Cape Town Dar es Salaam Hong Kong Karachi
Kuala Lumpur Madrid Melbourne Mexico City Nairobi
New Delhi Shanghai Taipei Toronto

With offices in

Argentina Austria Brazil Chile Czech Republic France Greece
Guatemala Hungary Italy Japan Poland Portugal Singapore
South Korea Switzerland Thailand Turkey Ukraine Vietnam

OXFORD and OXFORD ENGLISH are registered trademarks of
Oxford University Press

© Oxford University Press 2007

Database right Oxford University Press (maker)

Library of Congress Cataloging-in-Publication Data

Blackwell, Angela. Open Forum 1. / Angela M. Blackwell,
Therese Naber. p. cm.

Includes bibliographical references.

isbn-13: 978-0-19-436109-5 (student book)
isbn-13: 978-0-19-436110-1 (audio cd component)
isbn-13: 978-0-19-441777-8 (audio cassette component)
isbn-13: 978-0-19-441779-2 (answer key and test packet)

1. English language—Textbooks for foreign speakers. I. Title: Open Forum 1.
II. Naber, Therese. III. Title.

PE1128.B5844 2006
428.3'4—dc22   2005030682

Executive Publisher: Janet Aitchison
Senior Acquisitions Editor: Pietro Alongi
Editor: Rob Freire
Associate Editor: Scott Allan Wallick
Art Director: Maj-Britt Hagsted
Art Editor: Justine Eun
Production Manager: Shanta Persaud
Production Controller: Eve Wong

isbn-13: 978 0 19 436109-5
isbn-10: 0 19 436109-8

Printed in Hong Kong.

10 9 8 7 6 5 4 3 2 1

Photography Credits:

*The publishers would like to thank the following for their permission to reproduce
photographs:*
Alamy: BennetPhoto, 34 (archaeologist); Classic Image, 79 (Columbus);
Jarrod Erbe, 88 (euphorbia); Expuesto-Nicolas Randall, 34 (old
manuscript); Holt Studios International Ltd., 17 (cocoa tree); D. Hurst,
91 (laptop); Fergus Kennedy, 18 (Eden Project exterior); David L.
Moore, 73 (children swimming); Felipe Rodriguez, 60; Jack Sullivan,
18 (Eden Project interior); ChinaStock: 79 (Zheng He); Courtesy of the
Computer History Museum: 91 (old computer); CORBIS: Jack Fields, 34
(anthropologist);

Getty Images: AFP, 42; Digital Vision, 65 (Asian male); Hulton
Archive, 79 (Leif Erikson); Courtesy of Henry Holt and Company:
56; Jupiterimages Unlimited: Ablestock.com, 21 (flower, honey),
82 (Ellis Island); Brand X Images: 87 (calendar, clock), 88 (calla lily);
Comstock.com, 9 (laptop), 73 (irrigation); Creatas, 1 (man and child),
9 (newspaper), 73 (fishing), 87 (restaurant bill); Photos.com, 1 (hailing
taxi), 17 (rice field), 21 (bees), 60 (college students), 88 (trillium, wild
geranium); PhotoObjects.com, 87 (calculator); Pixland, 60 (family
dinner); Thinkstock, 65 (woman); Oxford University Press: 13 (Treasure
Island); Courtesy of Penguin Group, hc: 13 (The Catcher in the Rye);
Photodisc: Active Maturity: 65 (African-American male); Gretchen
Shields: 13 (The Joy Luck Club); SuperStock: Scott Barrow, Inc., 1 (air
traffic controller); Superstock, Inc.: 82 (immigrants).

Art Credits:

Matt Collins: 25, 47, 78; Marthe Roberts/Shea – Taxi Graphics, Inc.: 17,
41, 69.

The publishers would also like to thank the following for their help:

"The Telephone Penetrates American Households" graph reproduced
with permission of Simon & Schuster Adult Publishing Group from
Bowling Alone: The Collapse & Revival of American Community by Robert
D. Putnam. Copyright © 2000 by Robert D. Putnam

Acknowledgements

We would like to acknowledge Janet Aitchison and Pietro Alongi, who initiated the *Open Forum* series. We would also like to thank the editor, Rob Freire, and the design team at OUP for their hard work and dedication throughout the project. We would also like to express our gratitude to the following people for their support and feedback during the development of the series: Nigel Caplan, Jack Crow, Kate Dobiecka, Barbara Mattingly, Adrianne Ochoa, Ashli Totti, and Scott Allen Wallick. Special thanks to Deborah Pardes of the SIBL Project for her collaboration..

The publisher would like to thank the Hirshhorn Museum and Sculpture Garden, Smithsonian Institution, for permission to reproduce the following work:

Spiral Composition, 1946

Alexander Calder (1898–1976)

Gouache on paper (44.8 x 50.7 cm)

Hirshhorn Museum and Sculpture Garden, Smithsonian Institution, Gift of Joseph H. Hirshhorn, 1966.

Photographer: Lee Stalsworth.

Contents

Listening Skill Focus	Speaking Skill Focus	Vocabulary	Pronunciation
Reflecting on listening	Asking for help with vocabulary	Verbs of communication	Contractions with *be*
Activating background knowledge (1)	Reflecting on speaking	Words related to books	Stress on content words
Activating background knowledge (2)	Asking for clarification	Geographic areas and the definite article (*the*)	Unstressed function words
Predicting	Taking time to think	Verbs and adjectives with prepositions	Stressed and unstressed prepositions
Listening for main ideas	Clarifying	Nouns for professions	Word stress
Working out unknown vocabulary	Asking for further information	Words related to money	Intonation in lists
Identifying speculative language	Using expressions to show interest	Multi-word verbs (1)	Using intonation to show interest
Listening for specific information	Elaborating	Describing trends	Unstressed object pronouns
Identifying sequencers	Saying percentages and fractions	Collocations with *make* and *do*	Linking
Summarizing	Giving presentations	Multi-word verbs (2)	Unstressed and contracted auxiliary verbs
Listening for examples	Giving opinions and responding to opinions	Adjectives with *–ing* and *–ed* endings	The *–ed* ending
Identifying important points	Rephrasing to check understanding	The adjective endings *–al, –ent, –ive*	Intonation with *wh–* questions

Introduction

Welcome to *Open Forum,* a three-level listening and speaking skills series for English language learners who need practice in extended listening and discussion in preparation for academic work, or to attain a personal goal.

The series is structured around high-interest listening texts with an academic focus that engage and motivate learners. Chapters feature academic content areas such as History, Communication, or Psychology. The content areas are revisited as the series progresses, ensuring that learners recycle and extend the ideas and vocabulary of each topic. Focused practice in listening and speaking skills is integrated into each chapter.

Open Forum 1 is for learners at the **high-beginning** level.

Features of *Open Forum*

Listening Skills

- Each chapter introduces and practices a specific listening skill (e.g., listening for main ideas, identifying examples, identifying important points).

- Listening selections are adapted from authentic sources. They are carefully chosen to engage learners and teachers and to stimulate discussion.

- A wide variety of texts—including lectures, radio interviews, news reports, and informal conversations—ensures learners practice listening to a range of audio formats.

- Listening comprehension tasks provide opportunities for extensive and intensive listening, which becomes more challenging as learners move through the series.

Speaking Skills

- Each chapter introduces and practices one specific speaking skill (e.g., elaborating, asking for clarification, giving opinions).

- Speaking practice sections in each chapter provide opportunities for extended discussion on the chapter theme.

- Abundant opportunities for interaction in pairs, groups, and as a class ensure student participation.

Vocabulary

- Vocabulary sections introduce key lexical items associated with the chapter theme. The sections also highlight word-building, collocations, and multi-word verbs.

Pronunciation

- Pronunciation sections raise learners' awareness of features of natural spoken English, such as stress, rhythm, intonation, and linking.

MP3 Component

- Downloadable audio files (in MP3 format) and worksheets for every chapter are available on the *Open Forum* Web site www.oup.com/elt/openforum. Each downloadable selection complements the topic in the corresponding chapter, and provides learners with opportunities for extended listening practice in the content area. The listening selections can be used independently, or in a language lab setting.

Assessment

- Progress Tests (available in the *Answer Key* and *Test Booklet*) enable teachers to check learners' progress and allow learners to demonstrate mastery of the strategies they have studied.

Unit Format

1. Introducing the Topic

This section introduces the topic of the chapter, activates learners' background knowledge, and builds interest. Learners complete a quiz, answer discussion questions, look at photographs, or carry out a short survey.

> *Teaching Tip: Use this section to get learners thinking and speaking about the chapter theme. Have them work in pairs or groups to maximize their speaking opportunities.*

2. Listening Practice

This is the first of two major listening opportunities in each chapter. Each listening section includes five sub-sections:

- **Preparing to Listen**

  Here, learners are given specific preparation for the text that they are going to hear. Learners read and discuss information specific to the piece; at this point, new vocabulary may be introduced to facilitate listening.

  > *Teaching Tip: Heighten student interest and anticipation by having them predict what speakers will say. Leave some questions unanswered; this will motivate learners to listen more carefully.*

- **Listening for Main Ideas**

  This stage ensures that learners are able to identify the main idea of a text. The listening task encourages learners to listen to the entire recording once through, without stopping, and to pick out the general gist of the text.

  > *Teaching Tip: Read through the directions for the task before learners listen. Check that they understand the vocabulary in the task and know what they have to do. Encourage them to focus only on the listening task as they listen. After they listen, have learners compare their answers, and check as a class.*

■ Listening for More Detail

In this section, learners practice listening for specific details. As the series progresses, learners move from reacting with a minimal response (e.g., deciding whether a statement is true or false) to making more extended notes (e.g., filling in a chart). They are also guided to use context to work out unknown vocabulary.

Teaching Tip: Go through the questions before learners listen, and check that they understand what they are being asked. Then play the recording. Learners may already be able to answer some of the questions. Acknowledge this fact, but do not confirm right or wrong answers at this point: encourage learners to listen a second time to check their answers. After they have listened again, ask learners to compare their answers, and check as a class. If learners have difficulty with one or more of the questions, replay the relevant section of the recording as necessary.

■ Thinking and Speaking

At this point, learners are encouraged to respond to the ideas in the text, synthesize what they have heard, and apply it to their own experience. Learners also get an opportunity for speaking practice on the chapter theme.

Teaching Tip: Learners can discuss the questions in pairs, small groups, or as a class. Give them time to think before asking for answers. Encourage them to refer to the listening transcript if appropriate. The tasks are designed to be flexible and can take as little as a few minutes, or as long as 20–30 minutes, depending on class and teacher preference.

■ Focus on the Listening Skill

This section raises learners' awareness of listening skills and strategies, and provides focused training in those skills. The *Listening Skill* boxes introduce three types of listening skills:

a) pre-listening skills (e.g., activating background knowledge) are introduced before learners listen to the text;

b) while-listening skills (e.g., identifying main ideas) are introduced and practiced as learners listen;

c) detailed listening skills (e.g., working out unknown vocabulary) are practiced after learners have grasped the main points.

Teaching Tip: Read the information in the Listening Skill *box aloud as the learners follow along. Check that they understand. Then have them complete the tasks alone or with a partner. After they listen, have learners compare their answers, and check as a class.*

3. Vocabulary

The vocabulary section introduces key items of vocabulary that are useful for the topic, and provides written and oral practice of the items. Where necessary, *FYI* boxes highlight relevant information.

Teaching Tip: Read the information in the FYI *box, if there is one, aloud as the learners follow along. Check*

that learners understand. Then ask learners to complete the tasks alone or with a partner.

4. Listening Practice

This section provides a second listening opportunity. The text in this section is longer than the first text, to give learners practice in extended listening. The text is usually of a different type from the first text (e.g., a lecture vs. a radio interview). The sequence of tasks is the same as in the first listening section, without the specific focus on a listening skill.

Teaching Tip: See previous Listening Practice.

5. Pronunciation

Learners are offered practice in listening for and understanding features of natural spoken English such as stress, linking, weak forms, and verb endings. Learners practice focused listening to identify stress and intonation and to pick out words and complete sentences. As in the *Vocabulary* section, *FYI* boxes provide relevant instruction.

Teaching Tip: Read the information in the FYI *box, if there is one, aloud as the learners follow along. Check that learners understand. Then ask learners to complete the tasks alone or with a partner.*

6. Speaking Skills

This section raises learners' awareness of a specific speaking skill or strategy, such as asking for clarification or taking time to think. These are presented in *Speaking Skill* boxes. Learners listen to a short text that exemplifies the skill or strategy in question.

Teaching Tip: Read the information in the Speaking Skill *box aloud as the learners follow along. Check that learners understand. Then ask learners to complete the tasks alone or with partner.*

7. Speaking Practice

This section provides an extensive, guided speaking activity on the theme of the chapter, and encourages learners to use the skill learned in the previous section. The activity is carefully staged to maximize speaking; for example, learners might first make notes individually, then discuss the topic with a partner, and finally move into group or class discussion.

Teaching Tip: Allow plenty of time for this activity. Ask learners to gather and note down their ideas; this will ensure that they have enough to say in the speaking stage. If necessary, remind learners to use the speaking skill from the previous section.

8. Taking Skills Further

The chapter concludes with suggestions to increase learners' awareness of listening and speaking skills, and ideas for listening and speaking practice outside the classroom.

Teaching Tip: The task can usually be checked in the next class. Many of the activities can be expanded into a project, if desired.

ABOUT THIS CHAPTER

Topics:	Sign language; gestures
Listening Texts:	Radio report about babies and sign language; lecture about gestures
Listening Skill Focus:	Reflecting on listening
Speaking Skill Focus:	Asking for help with vocabulary
Vocabulary:	Verbs of communication
Pronunciation:	Contractions with *be*

1 INTRODUCING THE TOPIC

1. Work in small groups. Look at the pictures. How are the people communicating? What are they communicating in each picture?

2. Work in pairs or small groups. Make a list of other ways that people communicate without using words.

2 | LISTENING PRACTICE

A Preparing to Listen

You are going to listen to a radio report. Read the description of the report. Then discuss the questions with a partner.

Radio Highlights
WDLG 10:00: *Using sign language with babies*

This report investigates why parents are teaching their babies to use sign language before they can talk.

1. What is the radio report about?
2. What are some possible reasons that parents might teach babies to use sign language?

B Listening for Main Ideas

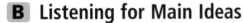 Listen to the radio report. Then choose the correct answer to the question.

What is the <u>main</u> reason that parents are learning to use sign language?
   a. They want to communicate with deaf people.
   b. They want to help their babies to communicate.
   c. They want their babies to speak earlier.

C Listening for More Detail

 Listen to the report again. As you listen, choose the correct answer to complete each statement. Then compare answers with a partner. Listen again if necessary.

1. The interview is taking place _____.
   a. at a radio station
   b. at a sign language class
   c. on a street corner

2. In the sign language classes, teachers teach signs to _____.
   a. babies
   b. parents
   c. researchers

3. The babies in the sign language class are _____.
   a. all the same age
   b. about two
   c. different ages

4. Parents like to use sign language because _____.
   a. it helps them understand what their children want
   b. it stops them from screaming at their children
   c. it stops the children from speaking

5. Researchers noticed that deaf children learn to sign _____.
   a. earlier than hearing children learn to speak
   b. more quickly than hearing children do
   c. later than hearing children do

6. Sign language may help children _____.
   a. become more intelligent
   b. learn to speak earlier
   c. both a. and b.

D Thinking and Speaking

Work in small groups and discuss the questions.

1. What are the advantages to teaching sign language to babies?

2. What do you think of the idea?

E Focus on the Listening Skill: Reflecting on Listening

> **LISTENING SKILL**
>
> It is helpful to think about the skills that are necessary to be a good listener. Thinking about these skills and practicing them as much as possible will improve your listening abilities and make you feel more confident when listening.

1. Work with a partner. Look at the listening situations below. For each pair of situations, discuss which type of listening is easier for you. Why is it easier? What kinds of listening situations are most difficult for you?

   1. Listening to a recording OR listening to someone face to face

   2. Listening in an informal situation (at a meal with friends) OR listening in a formal situation (in a lecture)

   3. Listening to a talk on a familiar topic OR listening to a talk on an unfamiliar topic

2. Look at these strategies for becoming a better listener. Then look back at sections A through D on pages 2 and 3. Which strategy did you use in each section?

1. Think about what you already know about the topic before you listen.
   _____Section A_____

2. Focus on the main ideas, not on the details. _____

3. Listen for specific information that you want to find out. _____

4. After you listen, try to summarize what you heard. _____

3. Look at the list of listening skills in the Table of Contents. Which chapters focus on the strategies above?

3 VOCABULARY: Verbs of Communication

Verbs of communication, like *say* or *tell*, are followed by different sentence structures. The chart below shows how some of these verbs are used in sentences.

	. . . to someone	. . . something to someone	. . . someone something or . . . someone about something
talk . . .	✔		
speak . . .	✔		
say . . .		✔	
explain . . .		✔	
tell . . .		✔	✔
ask . . .			✔

1. Read and listen to the conversation. Which verbs of communication do the speakers use?

A: Did you talk to Mike?

B: Yes. He explained why he was late for the meeting. He was sick.

A: He didn't say anything about a new job?

B: No. He told me he had the flu.

A: Hmm. That's strange.

2. Choose the correct answer to complete each statement. Use the chart on page 4 to help you.

1. My friend isn't speaking _____ because he's mad.
   a. me
   b. to me

2. He tells _____ all his problems.
   a. me
   b. to me

3. You never say _____.
   a. me hello
   b. hello to me

4. Could you please explain _____ again?
   a. me the homework
   b. the homework to me

5. When people are talking _____, I don't always understand.
   a. each other
   b. to each other

6. I'm going to ask _____ about the exam.
   a. the teacher
   b. to the teacher

3. Work with a partner. Discuss the following questions. Use some of the different communication verbs from the chart in your discussion.

1. Who do you talk to most often on the phone? Why?

2. What stories did your parents tell you when you were a child?

3. What would you like someone to explain to you?

4. If you met the President of the United States, what would you say?

4 LISTENING PRACTICE

A Preparing to Listen

1. Work with a partner. Describe how to do something, like how to get to your home from where you are now, how to make an unusual drink, or how to operate a motorcycle. As you speak, keep your hands behind your back and do not move your head!

2. Work in small groups and discuss the questions.

1. Is it difficult to speak without using hand or head movements?

2. How do a speaker's gestures help people understand him or her?

3. In what situations might you use more gestures than usual?

B Listening for Main Ideas

Read the statements. Then listen to the lecture by a university professor. As you listen, write *T* for true or *F* for false for each statement. Compare answers with a partner.

_____ 1. We learn to use hand movements by watching other people.

_____ 2. Gestures usually match what a person is saying.

_____ 3. Gestures help people put thoughts and ideas into speech.

C Listening for More Detail

Listen to the lecture again. Choose the correct answer to complete each sentence. Then compare answers with a partner. Listen again if necessary.

1. Professor Goldin-Meadow is _____.
   a. the person giving the lecture
   b. a researcher on the subject of gestures

2. The lecture is about _____.
   a. well-known gestures such as the "thumbs up" sign
   b. hand and eye movements that we use when we talk

3. Blind people make gestures. This shows that _____.
   a. it's harder for blind people to express themselves
   b. gestures are not learned from watching other people

4. The example of the "downstairs" gesture is an example of _____.
   a. a gesture that gives additional information that is not in the words
   b. a gesture that doesn't match the words

5. Goldin-Meadow studied children in order to see _____.
   a. how their hand movements are different from adults'
   b. when their hand movements didn't match their words

6. When people are speaking a foreign language or explaining something complicated, they often _____.
   a. use more gestures
   b. use gestures that don't match their words

D Thinking and Speaking

Work with a partner. Choose one of the following points from the lecture. Imagine that your partner did not hear the lecture, and explain the point in your own words, using examples from the lecture.

1. Gestures are not learned by watching people.

2. Gestures usually match what someone is saying.

3. Gestures help us put thoughts into words.

5 | PRONUNCIATION: Contractions with *Be*

> **FYI**
>
> It can be hard to hear the different forms of the word *be* (*am*, *is*, and *are*) because they are often contracted. For example, *I am* is contracted to *I'm*, and *he is* is contracted to *he's*.

🎧 1. **Read and listen to the sentence. Underline the three places where the verb *be* is contracted.**

When you're listening to people, it's interesting to pay attention to the gestures they're using.

🎧 2. **Listen to the extracts from the lecture. Fill in the missing contractions.**

1. It's something that we do naturally, and that _____*we're*_____ all born with.

2. And when we talk to each other, _____ paying attention to gestures as well.

3. You will automatically understand: "_____ in her office and her office is downstairs."

4. So usually _____ a correspondence, or a match, between the gestures a person makes and what they say in words.

5. People use more gestures when they have difficulty with language, for example,

   when _____ speaking a foreign language.

6. It can tell you a lot about _____ going on in their heads.

6 | SPEAKING SKILL: Asking for Help with Vocabulary

> **SPEAKING SKILL**
>
> When you are speaking, it is sometimes difficult to think of the right word. If you cannot remember a word, try one or more of the strategies below to get help.
> - Describe what you mean using a similar word or gesture.
> - Use a more general word.
> - Use an expression like "What do you call it?"
> - Give part of the word and ask for help.

🎧 1. **Listen to the conversation. What is the woman describing?**

🎧 2. **Listen again. Which of the strategies above does the woman use?**

7 | SPEAKING PRACTICE

Work in small groups. Take turns thinking of an item from the categories listed below. Describe the item as clearly as you can. Do not use the name of the item. Instead, use the strategies on page 7 to ask for help. How quickly can your classmates guess the item you are describing?

| an animal | a color | a fruit or vegetable |
| clothing or jewelry | a feeling | a type of music |

Example:

A: It's a kind of fruit . . . and it's green on the outside. What do you call it?

B: Do you mean a pear . . . or maybe an apple?

A: No. It's bigger . . . about this big.

C: Oh, a watermelon!

A: Right!

8 | TAKING SKILLS FURTHER

In a conversation outside of class, when you cannot think of a word, try using one or more of the strategies for asking for help. Discuss your experiences in the next class.

 For additional listening practice on the topic of communication, go to the *Open Forum* Web site (www.oup.com/elt/openforum) and follow the links.

ABOUT THIS CHAPTER

Topics:	Literacy and reading
Listening Texts:	Interview about Artists for Literacy; informal conversation about books
Listening Skill Focus:	Activating background knowledge (1)
Speaking Skill Focus:	Reflecting on speaking
Vocabulary:	Words related to books
Pronunciation:	Stress on content words

1 | **INTRODUCING THE TOPIC**

1. Look at the list of reading materials. Number the materials 1–5 according to how often you read each type (1 = the most often, 5 = the least often).

   _____ textbooks or academic texts

   _____ newspapers

   _____ magazines

   _____ online material (e-mail, blogs, online magazines)

   _____ nonacademic books (mystery stories, novels)

2. Work in small groups. Compare your answers. What kind of material do you most enjoy reading?

3. Write a list of everything that you have read so far today. Include things like road signs and advertisements. Then compare your answers in small groups. How many different things did your group read?

2 | LISTENING PRACTICE

A Focus on the Listening Skill: Activating Background Knowledge (1)

> **LISTENING SKILL**
>
> Before you listen to a talk or a program about a topic, think about what you already know about the topic. Even if you do not know much about it, just thinking about it in advance will help you prepare for what you are going to hear.

You are going to hear a radio interview about an organization called Artists for Literacy. Before listening, discuss these questions with a partner.

1. Many children do not read well even after graduating from high school. How does the ability to read and write well affect a student's future?

2. How can teachers and parents encourage students to read more?

3. What do you think the organization Artists for Literacy might do?

B Listening for Main Ideas

Listen to the interview. Then choose the correct answer to the question.

What does the organization Artists for Literacy do?
- a. It raises money for literacy programs.
- b. It provides tutors to help children learn to read.
- c. It provides songs for teachers to use to encourage students to read.

C Listening for More Detail

Listen to the interview again. As you listen, circle the correct word or phrase to complete each statement. Then compare answers with a partner. Listen again if necessary.

1. Statistics show that the top 2 percent of students in the United States read for 20 / 65 minutes a day.

2. It's hard to get children to read because they can't read well / they prefer to watch TV or listen to music.

3. The artists that Gwyneth Dunne mentions have all written novels, stories, or poems / songs inspired by literature.

4. In the classroom, teachers usually have students listen to the songs and then read the book / read the book and then listen to the songs.

5. In a recent project, the students made their own paintings / wrote their own songs about a novel they had read.

6. The project started when the founder of the organization heard a program about a book / performed a song she had written on the radio.

D Thinking and Speaking

Discuss these questions in small groups.

1. What do you think of using music to get students interested in reading?

2. What other ways could teachers use art to inspire children to read books?

3. What makes you want to read a book?

3 VOCABULARY: Words Related to Books

1. Read the book descriptions. Pay attention to the words in bold.

OUR STAFF RECOMMMENDS...

Wait until Tomorrow

*Carrie Jones's **best-seller** has finally been released in **paperback**. This is a mystery story with an intricate **plot**. You never know what will happen next! A real page-turner. I couldn't put it down.*

Hannah on the Farm

*This classic of children's literature was first **published** in 1912 but the timeless story of the little girl on the farm is just as enjoyable today. This **edition** has beautiful **illustrations** of all the farmyard **characters**. Recommended for ages 5 to 8.*

Meditations for Everyday

*A tiny book of poetry and short stories on the eternal **themes** of love, life, and death. Inspirational reading!*

The Prisoner of Dromore

*This is a **sequel** to Finding Dromore, and the final **novel** in the Dromore **series**, The story of life in a small town continues as a generation grows up and looks toward the future.*

Headed West

*The true story of how the West was won. Awarded the Newton prize for **nonfiction**.*

2. Try to match each word on the left with a definition on the right. Then compare answers with a partner.

_c_	1. best-seller	a.	to produce reading material for sale
____	2. paperback	b.	a story that is long enough to fill a complete book
____	3. plot	c.	a book that is bought by a large number of people
____	4. publish	d.	writing that describes real people and events
____	5. edition	e.	a book that has a paper cover
____	6. illustrations	f.	a book that continues the story of an earlier one
____	7. character	g.	a set of books with the same characters or the same subject
____	8. theme	h.	the form or version in which a book is published
____	9. sequel	i.	the events that form the story of a book
____	10. novel	j.	a person or animal in a book
____	11. series	k.	a subject or main idea in a book
____	12. nonfiction	l.	drawings or pictures in a book

3. Look at the following categories. List as many examples for each category as you can think of. Then work in small groups and compare your answers. Did you think of the same examples?

1. A current best-seller: _____

_____

2. A paperback novel that you recently read: _____

_____

3. A character in a well-known book: _____

_____

4. A book or movie with an exciting plot: _____

_____

5. A book or movie that is a sequel, or part of a series: _____

_____

A Preparing to Listen

Work in small groups. Look at the three books and their descriptions. Discuss the questions.

interconnected stories about Chinese American mothers and daughters in San Francisco

a classic novel about an alienated teenager growing up in New York

a timeless adventure story about pirates, buried treasure, and danger

1. Have you read any of these books?

2. If you have read one or more of the books, what do you remember about them?

3. Which one looks most interesting to you? Why?

B Listening for Main Ideas

 Anne, Cora, and Brent are discussing these books. Listen to their conversation and note the main reason why each book is important to the person who describes it.

1. *The Joy Luck Club* (Anne) _____

2. *The Catcher in the Rye* (Cora) _____

3. *Treasure Island* (Brent) _____

C Listening for More Detail

 Read the statements. Then listen to the conversation again. Write *T* for true or *F* for false for each statement. Compare answers with a partner.

Anne

_____ 1. Before reading *The Joy Luck Club*, she had never read a book about Chinese Americans.

_____ 2. Her father comes from China.

_____ 3. After she read the book, she became more interested in her own background.

_____ 4. She didn't see the movie.

Cora

_____ 5. She identified with the main character in *The Catcher in the Rye*.

_____ 6. She thought the main character was dishonest.

_____ 7. She had to read the book for school.

_____ 8. Before reading the book, she was not usually interested in English classes.

Brent

_____ 9. He found *Treasure Island* at his home.

_____ 10. He read the book every day.

_____ 11. He read the book more than once.

_____ 12. He didn't understand the illustrations.

D Thinking and Speaking

Work with a partner. Discuss the questions.

At the end of the conversation, Anne says, "That's why books are so great for kids. They open up a whole world of possibilities to you." What do you think she means? What kinds of possibilities can books open up for children?

5 PRONUNCIATION: Stress on Content Words

 In spoken English, content words (nouns, verbs, adjectives, or adverbs), such as *Anne*, *reads*, *good*, or *quickly*, are usually stressed. Function words (articles, prepositions, or conjunctions), such as *the*, *in*, or *but*, are usually unstressed.

1. **Read and listen to the sentences. Note how the speaker stresses the content words.**

   1. I **read** a **good book.**

   2. It was **written** by **Amy Tan.**

   3. I was **interested** in **China.**

   4. My **father** was **born** there.

2. **Read the sentences and underline the words that you think will be stressed. Then listen and check your answers.**

   1. We visited my grandparents in Brooklyn.

   2. I found a great book.

   3. There were pictures of pirates.

   4. The illustrations were beautiful.

   5. I read it on Sundays.

6 | SPEAKING PRACTICE

1. Prepare to describe a book that you enjoyed, or one that you remember well.
   Read the questions about the book and write your answers in the chart below.

   1. Title of the book: _____

   2. Where and when does the story take place? _____

   3. Who is / are the main character / characters? _____

   4. What is the plot? (What happens in the book? What is the story?)

      _____

      _____

   5. Who are some of the other characters in the book, and how do they affect the

      story? _____

      _____

   6. Does it have a happy or a sad ending? _____

   7. Why did you like the book? (Was it interesting, amusing, exciting, sad?)

      _____

      _____

   8. Who would you recommend the book to? _____

2. Work in small groups. Take turns describing your book to the group. Then
   decide which of the other books you would be most interested in reading, and
   say why.

7 | SPEAKING SKILLS: Reflecting on Speaking

SPEAKING SKILL

It is helpful to think about the speaking situations you often face
and the difficulties you sometimes have in these situations. It is
also helpful to learn some strategies to use when you have difficulty
communicating in these common situations.

1. Work with a partner. Look at the list of speaking situations. Match each situation with the skill or strategy (a–e below) that you think would be most helpful in that situation. Can you think of other situations where the skill or strategy would be useful?

   1. I asked someone for directions, but I didn't understand part of the answer.

      Useful skill or strategy: <u>b. Asking for clarification</u>

   2. The teacher asked me a question in class, but I couldn't think of an answer right away.

      Useful skill or strategy: _____

   3. The teacher put us in small groups to discuss the importance of advertising.

      Useful skill or strategy: _____

   4. I wanted some more information about the test next week.

      Useful skill or strategy: _____

   5. My friend was telling me a story about his family and I didn't know how to respond.

      Useful skill or strategy: _____

   a. Asking for further information
   b. Asking for clarification
   c. Expressing interest
   d. Expressing opinions
   e. Taking time to think

2. Look at the list of speaking skills in the Table of Contents at the front of the book. Which chapters deal with the speaking skills and strategies above?

3. Which speaking skills and strategies do you feel are most important for you to learn? Why?

8 | TAKING SKILLS FURTHER

Next time you listen to a lecture, a radio program, or a TV news program, practice activating background knowledge. Think about the topic in advance and what you already know about it. Talk about your experiences in the next class.

 For additional listening practice on the topic of literature, go to the *Open Forum* Web site (www.oup.com/elt/openforum) and follow the links.

CHAPTER 3 Life Sciences

1 | INTRODUCING THE TOPIC

1. Work with a partner. Discuss possible answers to the quiz. (The answers are at the bottom of the page.)

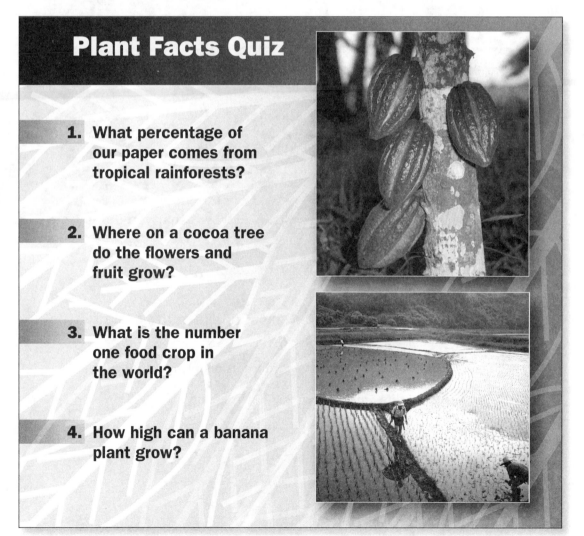

Plant Facts Quiz

1. What percentage of our paper comes from tropical rainforests?

2. Where on a cocoa tree do the flowers and fruit grow?

3. What is the number one food crop in the world?

4. How high can a banana plant grow?

Answers: 1. 1%; 2. on the trunk and branches; 3. rice; 4. 35 feet high

2. Work in groups. Make a list of everyday items that come from plants. Think about foods, drinks, fabrics, materials for building houses, etc. Then compare your answers with a partner.

2 | LISTENING PRACTICE

A Focus on the Listening Skill: Activating Background Knowledge (2)

> **LISTENING SKILL**
>
> Before you listen to a talk or a program about a topic, think of some words and expressions that are connected to the topic. This will help you prepare for what you are going to hear.

1. Work with a partner. Look at the photos of the Eden Project and make a list of any words or expressions you know related to plants and gardens.

2. Work in small groups. Compare your lists. Add words that you did not have on your list.

B Listening for Main Ideas

You are going to listen to a tour guide talk about the Eden Project. After listening, mark the one statement that is false.

_____ 1. The Eden Project has gardens and educates people about horticulture.

_____ 2. There are four different landscape and garden areas.

_____ 3. The plants were not taken from the wild.

C Listening for More Detail

 Listen to the talk again. Choose the correct answer to complete each statement. Then compare answers with a partner. Listen again if necessary.

1. The tour guide says the Eden Project wants to make issues related to plants _____.
   a. interesting to anyone
   b. interesting to people who work with plants

2. The Eden Project has _____.
   a. 5000 different plants
   b. 100,000 different plants

3. The Eden Project has _____.
   a. three different biomes
   b. two different biomes

4. The different areas of the Eden Project are _____.
   a. an outdoor landscape, a temperate biome, and a tropical biome
   b. a temperate biome and a tropical biome

5. Each section has _____.
   a. only plants used for food
   b. different types of plants used for food, clothing, and other things

6. The outdoor landscape area has plants from _____.
   a. Britain
   b. Britain, Russia, and parts of North and South America

7. The warm temperate biome has plants that live in places where _____.
   a. it's dry and the soil isn't good
   b. it's dry but the soil is good

8. The humid tropics biome _____.
   a. is the largest in the country
   b. is the largest in the world

D Thinking and Speaking

Work in pairs or small groups. Discuss the questions.

1. Do you think the Eden Project's goals (education about plants and conservation) are important? Why or why not?

2. What other projects that conserve plants or animals do you know of? Describe them.

3 | VOCABULARY: Geographic Areas and the Definite Article (*The*)

 Certain names for geographic areas use the definite article *the*. These include oceans, seas, rivers, mountain ranges, and groups of islands. We also use *the* with place names that include a noun like *republic, state,* or *union,* for example, *The United States* or *The Czech Republic.*

1. **Read the extracts from the talk. Look at the underlined place names. Which two use the definite article (*the*)?**

   The outdoor landscape has the natural landscapes and plants of temperate regions, like most of <u>Britain</u> as well as parts of <u>Russia</u> and parts of <u>North</u> and <u>South America</u>.

   For the warm temperate biome, think of the regions of <u>the Mediterranean</u>, as well as parts of <u>South Africa</u>, <u>Australia</u>, and some of <u>California</u> in <u>the United States</u>.

   For the humid tropics biome, think of tropical regions such as <u>West Africa</u>, <u>Malaysia</u>, and tropical <u>South America</u>.

2. **Work with a partner. Match each geographic category on the left (1–9) with a name on the right (a–i). Which names use the definite article?**

_f_ 1. continent	a.	The Atlantic
___ 2. country	b.	France
___ 3. a group of islands	c.	Mt. Everest
___ 4. lake	d.	Superior
___ 5. mountain	e.	The Mississippi
___ 6. mountain range	f.	Africa
___ 7. ocean	g.	The Himalayas
___ 8. sea	h.	The Caribbean
___ 9. river	i.	The Canaries

3. **Write another example for each category below.**

   Continent: _____ Europe _____

   Country: _____

   Group of islands: _____

   Lake: _____

   Mountain: _____

Mountain range: _____

Ocean: _____

Sea: _____

River: _____

4. Work with a partner. Take turns saying your examples from exercise 3. When your partner says an example, respond with the appropriate category.

> Example:
> Student A: *Europe*
> Student B: *A continent*

4 LISTENING PRACTICE

A Preparing to Listen

Work in pairs or in small groups. Look at the pictures and discuss how you think they are related.

B Listening for Main Ideas

Listen to a lecture about bees. Number the topics in the order they are mentioned.

_____ How the bee carries nectar

_____ Bee communication

_____ Structure of the hive

_____ How many kinds of bees there are

_____ How bees make honey

C Listening for More Detail

Listen to the lecture again. Write *T* for true or *F* for false for each statement. Then compare answers with a partner. Listen again if necessary.

_____ 1. Bees can only survive in warm places.

_____ 2. There are 2200 different kinds of bees that have been named.

_____ 3. A female worker bee goes to different flowers to collect nectar.

_____ 4. Only one bee works on the nectar to make it into honey.

_____ 5. The kind of flower the nectar comes from affects the flavor of the honey.

_____ 6. The worker bee carries nectar in a bag on its stomach.

_____ 7. The hive has two different kinds of bees in it.

_____ 8. Most bees in a hive are drones.

_____ 9. Bees communicate about the location, quantity, and quality of food.

_____ 10. Bees communicate by moving their bodies in a certain pattern.

D Thinking and Speaking

Work with a partner. Use information from the lecture to explain how bees make honey and how they communicate. Then answer the questions.

1. What new information did you learn from listening to the class?

2. What other animals communicate? How do they communicate?

5 | PRONUNCIATION: Unstressed Function Words

FYI

Some very common words, such as articles (*a, an, the*), prepositions (*to, of, on, from, at, in*), pronouns (*it, him, her*), and conjunctions (*and, or, as*) are usually unstressed in both formal and informal speech. They can be difficult to hear because they are unstressed.

1. Read and listen to the sentence. Pay attention to the words in italics. All these words are unstressed.

> You probably think *of* bees *in* warm places, *but* they actually survive *in* all kinds *of* places.

2. Listen to the extract from the lecture. Fill in the missing words. Then compare answers with a partner. Listen again if necessary.

> It turns out that bees can communicate (1) __to__ some extent. They can
>
> actually let other bees know about (2) _____ location (3) _____ food, not
>
> just where (4) _____ is, but how good (5) _____ is (6) _____ how
>
> much there is. The bees do (7) _____ kind (8) _____ dance, moving around
>
> (9) _____ (10) _____ air.

3. Work with a partner. Practice reading the extract aloud. Remember not to stress the words you filled in.

6 | SPEAKING SKILLS: Asking for Clarification

SPEAKING SKILL

After listening to someone speak, you may need to ask for clarification. Use the expressions below to help you get the clarification you need.

> Can you repeat . . . ?
> Could you repeat . . . ?
> Can you explain how . . . ?
> How many . . . ?
> What did you say about . . . ?

1. Listen to three questions that students ask during the lecture. What do they ask about?

2. Listen again. Which expressions do the speakers use?

1. Work with a partner. Student A: Cover text B and read text A. Student B: Cover text A and read text B. Some information is missing from each text. Ask your partner questions to complete the missing information in your text. Ask for clarification when necessary.

   Example:
   Student A: *Where did the honeybee originally come from?*
   Student B: *Africa.*

A.

FASCINATING FACTS ABOUT BEES

Most researchers believe the honeybee originally came from (1.) _____.

The average American eats about one pound of honey a year.

In the course of her lifetime, a worker bee will produce (2.)_____ of honey.

To make one pound of honey, workers in a hive fly 55,000 miles and visit

(3.) _____flowers.

In one trip, a worker will visit between 50 and 100 flowers.

A hive can make (4.) _____of honey a day.

The average speed a honeybee flies is 15 miles per hour.

There are (5.) _____ different kinds of bees in North America.

Bees can see colors, but not the color red.

B.

FASCINATING FACTS ABOUT BEES

Most researchers believe the honeybee originally came from Africa.

The average American eats (6.) _____ of honey a year.

In the course of her lifetime, a worker bee will produce 1/12th of a teaspoon of honey.

To make one pound of honey, workers in a hive fly (7.) _____
miles and visit two million flowers.

In one trip, a worker will visit between (8.) _____ flowers.

A hive can make two pounds of honey a day.

The average speed a honeybee flies is (9.) _____ per hour.

There are 4000 different kinds of bees in North America.

Bees can see colors, but not the color (10.) _____.

8 | TAKING SKILLS FURTHER

Listen to people talking outside of class. Pay attention to the ways people ask for clarification. Notice which expressions they use. Report your findings in the next class.

For additional listening practice on the topic of nature and biology, go to the *Open Forum* Web site (www.oup.com/elt/openforum) and follow the links.

ABOUT THIS CHAPTER

Topics:	The brain and memory
Listening Texts:	TV program about how to improve memory; radio call-in show
Listening Skill Focus:	Predicting
Speaking Skill Focus:	Taking time to think
Vocabulary:	Verbs and adjectives with prepositions
Pronunciation:	Stressed and unstressed prepositions

 1 **INTRODUCING THE TOPIC**

1. Look at the picture for 60 seconds. Then close your book and write down as many details as you remember from the picture.

2. Work with a partner. Compare your lists. How much did each of you remember? How easy or difficult was it for you to remember details?

A Focus on the Listening Skill: Predicting

LISTENING SKILL

Before you listen to any kind of lecture or talk, try to predict what it might be about. Look at the title and any visual material, such as pictures or handouts. Think about what someone might say or write about the topic. Even if your predictions are not correct, this can help prepare you for what you will hear.

1. Work with a partner. Look at the title for a TV news program. Then discuss the questions.

9:00 pm on Channel 6

Science Watch
What is "Boot Camp for the Brain" and how might it help you improve your memory?

1. Boot camp is a training program for people in the military. It usually involves rigorous physical activity. What might a boot camp for the brain involve?

2. What are some different kinds of memory problems that people have?

3. Why might someone want to improve his or her memory?

2. Look at the list of topics. Check the ones you think might be discussed in the news report.

_____ Examples of memory problems

_____ What happens at Boot Camp for the Brain

_____ Childhood memories

_____ A research study

_____ What other scientists think

_____ Using memory to prepare for college exams

B Listening for Main Ideas

 Listen to the TV news report about the Boot Camp for the Brain. As you listen, underline the topics above that are discussed.

C Listening for More Detail

 Listen to the report again. As you listen, choose the correct answer to complete each statement. Then compare answers with a partner. Listen again if necessary.

1. The Boot Camp for the Brain is _____.
   a. a two-week program
   b. a two-month program
   c. a three-week program

2. The program includes _____.
   a. only memory exercises
   b. memory exercises and a special diet
   c. memory exercises, a special diet, physical activity, and stress-relieving exercises

3. After the program, memory tests showed Michele Rubin's memory to be _____.
   a. average for her age
   b. equal to a 40-year-old person
   c. equal to a 20-year-old person

4. As a way to exercise her brain, Michele Rubin now helps her children with _____.
   a. math puzzles
   b. their math homework
   c. their reading homework

5. Dr. Small's study showed that people who did the program had _____.
   a. more efficiency in the front of their brains
   b. more efficiency in the back of their brains
   c. more efficiency in all of their brains

6. Other scientists feel that _____.
   a. the program definitely works
   b. the program doesn't work
   c. the program might work, but there needs to be more research

D Thinking and Speaking

Work with a partner. Explain in your own words how Boot Camp for the Brain works and Ms. Rubin's experience with it. Then discuss your opinion of the program. Do you think it could be helpful? Why or why not?

3 | VOCABULARY: Verbs and Adjectives with Prepositions

FYI Some verbs and adjectives commonly appear with certain prepositions. For example, the verb *think* usually goes with *about*, and the adjective *similar* usually goes with *to*. It is a good idea to learn some of these common combinations.

1. Read the brochure. Then complete the chart with the correct prepositions.

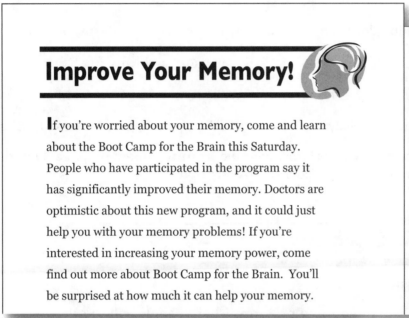

Improve Your Memory!

If you're worried about your memory, come and learn about the Boot Camp for the Brain this Saturday. People who have participated in the program say it has significantly improved their memory. Doctors are optimistic about this new program, and it could just help you with your memory problems! If you're interested in increasing your memory power, come find out more about Boot Camp for the Brain. You'll be surprised at how much it can help your memory.

Verb + Preposition	Adjective + Preposition
think about	similar to
wait for	different from
listen to	aware of
talk about	worried _____
talk to	optimistic _____
participate _____	interested _____
help (someone) _____	surprised _____

2. **Fill in the blanks with the correct prepositions.**

My father is worried (1) ___about___ his memory, and he's very interested (2) _____

learning about ways to improve it. So last week we went to a lecture on the brain and

memory. The lecture started with a psychologist talking (3) _____ the brain and

how memory works. My father listened (4) _____ the speaker and took notes

to remember the important points. In the second part of the lecture, we were asked

to participate (5) _____ memory tests. I was a little surprised (6) _____ my

results because I didn't do as well as I'd expected! After the tests, the psychologist

talked (7) _____ ways to help (8) _____ memory problems. My father felt

more optimistic (9) _____ his memory after the lecture, but I was a little worried

(10) _____ mine. Especially when I realized I'd forgotten where I'd parked the car!

3. **Work with a partner. Say a verb or adjective from the chart on page 29 and
   see if your partner can say the correct preposition.**

4 | LISTENING PRACTICE

A Preparing to Listen

1. You are going to listen to a radio program where people call to ask a
   psychologist about memory problems. Before you listen, work with a partner
   and make a list of problems that you think listeners might ask about.

2. Work in small groups and compare lists. What advice do you think a
   psychologist might give for the problems on your lists?

B Listening for Main Ideas

Read the following list of problems listeners ask about. Then listen and number
the problems in the order they are discussed.

_____ Ways to improve memory

_____ Forgetting names

_____ Tip of the tongue syndrome

_____ Stress and memory

C Listening for More Detail

Read the questions and answer the ones you can. Then listen to the radio show again and complete your answers. Compare answers with a partner. Listen again if necessary.

1. If you are worried about your memory, how does that affect your ability to remember things? _____

2. What is the main goal of any techniques to remember names?

   _____

3. What example is given to try and remember the name John Hatfield?

   _____

4. Why is it good to make the image for remembering a name silly or strange?

   _____

5. What are some different ways mentioned to give your brain a work out?

   _____

6. What is the tip of the tongue syndrome? _____

   _____

7. What does the psychologist suggest if, for example, you can't remember the name of a movie? _____

8. Why does she say this approach is helpful?

   _____

D Thinking and Speaking

Work in small groups and discuss the questions.

1. Have you ever tried any of these techniques to help your memory? If so, which ones?

2. Have you tried any other memory techniques?

3. Which technique would you like to try?

5 | PRONUNCIATION: Stressed and Unstressed Prepositions

FYI Prepositions can be stressed or unstressed, depending on the situation. Prepositions within a sentence are not usually stressed. If the preposition is at the end of the sentence or at the end of a question, it is usually stressed.

1. Listen to the questions in column 1 and the sentences in column 2. Are the prepositions in column 1 stressed or unstressed? How about in column 2?

Column 1	Column 2
What are you waiting for?	I'm waiting for a friend.
What's he looking at?	He's looking at some old photographs.
What are they listening to?	They're listening to a lecture about memory.
What's she interested in?	She's interested in science.

2. Listen to the questions and sentences again. Repeat each one with appropriate stress.

3. Work with a partner. Take turns asking and answering the questions below using appropriate stress.

1. Where are you from?
2. What are you interested in?
3. What do you hate waiting for?
4. What kind of music do you listen to?
5. What do you worry about?

6 | SPEAKING SKILLS: Taking Time to Think

SPEAKING SKILL

Don't worry if you need to stop and take time to think or remember something when you are speaking. When you do this, it's a good idea to say something to avoid silence. The expressions below can give you time to think.

Hmm . . .	Let me think . . .
Well . . .	Give me a second . . .
Let's see . . .	It's on the tip of my tongue . . .

1. Listen to the conversation. What are they talking about?

2. Listen again. Which expressions do the speakers use to take time to think?

1. Read the questionnaire. Then add two or three more questions about memory.

How's your memory?

1. What is your earliest memory?

2. How many different telephone numbers do you have memorized?

3. How many of your family and friends' birthdays can you remember

4. Do you remember names or faces better?

5. _____

_____

_____

_____

6. _____

_____

_____

_____

7. _____

_____

_____

_____

2. Work with a partner. Take turns asking and answering the questions. Make notes of your partner's answers.

3. Compare answers as a class. Which areas of memory do most people find easiest or most difficult?

8 | TAKING SKILLS FURTHER

Listen to people speaking outside of class. Notice when they stop to think about something while they are speaking. What expressions to do they use? Discuss your findings in the next class.

For additional listening practice on the topic of the brain and memory, go to the *Open Forum* Web site (www.oup.com/elt/openforum) and follow the links.

CHAPTER 5

Anthropology

ABOUT THIS CHAPTER

Topic:	Anthropology
Listening Texts:	Interview with an anthropologist; news report on corporate anthropology
Listening Skill Focus:	Listening for main ideas
Speaking Skill Focus:	Clarifying
Vocabulary:	Nouns for professions
Pronunciation:	Word stress

1 | INTRODUCING THE TOPIC

1. Work with a partner. Look at the pictures. Then discuss the questions.

   1. What do you think these people are doing?

   2. What do the pictures have in common?

2. Compare your answers in small groups.

2 | LISTENING PRACTICE

A Preparing to Listen

Read the description of anthropologists on the next page. Then work in small groups and discuss the questions.

Anthropologists are careful observers of humans and their behavior. They ask questions like: What does it mean to be human? Why do people behave in particular ways? What are universal facts of human life?

Science Today **15**

1. What exactly do you think anthropologists do? Where do you think they typically work?
2. What skills do you think a good anthropologist needs?
3. What kind of classes do you think you might take for a degree in anthropology?
4. Do you think anthropologists are paid well? Why or why not?

B Focus on the Listening Skill: Listening for Main Ideas

> **LISTENING SKILL**
>
> When you listen to a talk or a program for the first time, listen for the main ideas. Do not try to listen for every detail.

Read the statements. Then listen to the interview. After you listen, check the four main ideas presented in the interview. (All the ideas are mentioned.)

_____ Anthropology is the study of humans now or at any time in the past.

_____ The field of anthropology is generally divided into four areas.

_____ One area of study for cultural anthropologists is the customs of groups of people.

_____ Dr. Tate studies early music in North America.

_____ Dr. Tate suggests taking an introductory course and talking to people to find out about the field.

_____ Dr. Tate says an anthropologist is unlikely to get rich, but that it's a fascinating field.

C Listening for More Detail

 Read the questions and answer the ones you can. Then listen to the interview again and complete your answers. Compare answers with a partner.

1. What is studied in cultural anthropology? _____

2. What is studied in physical or biological anthropology? _____

3. What is studied in archaeology? _____

4. What is studied in linguistic anthropology? _____

5. What area is Dr. Tate working in now? _____

6. What does he think will happen in the field in the future? _____

_____

D Thinking and Speaking

Work in small groups. Discuss the questions.

1. What did you learn about anthropology that you did not know before?

2. Would you like to be an anthropologist? Why or why not?

3 VOCABULARY: Nouns for Professions

FYI Different suffixes are used to name a person who works in a certain profession. For example, the suffix –er is used to say that someone who *sings* is a *singer*, or –ian is used to show that someone who works in the field of *mathematics* is a *mathematician*.

1. Read the definitions. Underline the suffixes used to name the person who works in each profession.

1. A professional is someone who works in a profession.

2. An archaeologist is an expert in archaeology.

3. An actor is someone who acts on TV or in plays or movies.

4. A musician is someone whose job is to play a musical instrument.

5. A manager is a person who manages an organization or part of an organization.

2. Look back at the words with an underlined suffix. Add each word to the correct category in the chart. Then work with a partner to think of one or two more examples to add to each category.

–ist	–ian	–al	–or	–er
anthropologist artist	mathematician politician	official	professor director	employer

3. Use words from the chart to complete the statements.

1. My cousin is very good at mathematics. She's studying to be a _____.

2. Lou can draw and paint beautifully. Maybe he should be an _____.

3. The _____ of a movie tells the actors what to do.

4. Where do you work? Who is your _____?

5. I don't think I'd want to be a _____. The world of politics seems difficult.

6. There's a new biology _____ at my university. They say he's a very good teacher.

4 | LISTENING PRACTICE

A | Preparing to Listen

You are going to listen to a report about changes in the field of anthropology. Read the introduction to the report. Then discuss the introduction with a partner. What kind of work might an anthropologist do in an office?

Monday Evening News
Science Segment, page 2

Molly: When you think of an anthropologist, you probably think of someone who goes off to study a community that is far away and often very remote. That may have been true for anthropologists in the past, but things are changing. Today, while you still may find anthropologists who travel halfway around the world for their work, you might also be surprised to find one working just down the hall in your office.

B Listening for Main Ideas

🎧 Work with a partner. Listen to the report about corporate anthropology. Then answer the questions.

1. According to Sara Patton, how is her work in corporate settings similar to her previous work?

2. What is an example of something an anthropologist might do or study in a company?

C Listening for More Detail

🎧 Listen to the report again. As you listen, choose the correct answer to complete each statement. Then compare answers with a partner. Listen again if necessary.

1. Using anthropologists in the business world started as an experiment in _____.
   a. many companies
   b. a few companies
   c. one company

2. Anthropologists working in a company use _____.
   a. the same skills they would use in other situations
   b. the same skills but with extra skills as well
   c. different skills from the ones they use in other situations

3. Sara Patton _____.
   a. has always worked in corporate situations
   b. worked in a village near the Arctic Circle
   c. traveled to the Arctic Circle for the job she has now

4. In her current project, she is studying the group dynamics of _____.
   a. managers in an office
   b. workers in an office
   c. workers in a factory

5. A colleague of Sara's _____.
   a. observes how people use technology in their homes
   b. asks people how they use technology in their homes
   c. asks people how they use e-mail

6. Companies might use the information from Sara's colleague to _____.
   a. improve products
   b. design new products
   c. improve products and/or design new ones

D Thinking and Speaking

Work in small groups. Discuss the questions.

1. Do you think using anthropologists in business is a good idea? Why or why not?

2. In what other ways could companies get information about their customers?

5 | PRONUNCIATION: Word Stress

 Multi-syllable words have main stress on one syllable. The stress goes on the syllable before the suffix with these suffixes: *–ogy, –ogist, –ion, –ity.*

1. **Listen to the words. Notice which syllable is stressed in each word.**

   1. anthro**pol**ogy
   2. anthro**pol**ogist
   3. documen**ta**tion
   4. com**mun**ity

2. **Underline the stressed syllable in each word. Then listen and check your answers.**

   1. biology
   2. biologist
   3. archaeology
   4. archaeologist
   5. corporation
   6. observation
   7. personality
   8. quality

3. **Work with a partner. Practice saying the words in exercise 2 with the correct stress.**

6 | SPEAKING SKILL: Clarifying

SPEAKING SKILL

It is sometimes necessary to clarify what you have said in a conversation. Use the expressions below to show that you are clarifying. You can also restate what you have said to help clarify.

> In other words, . . .
>
> I mean . . .
>
> What I mean is . . .
>
> That's not what I meant. . . .
>
> No, I said . . .

1. Listen to the conversation. What are the speakers discussing?

2. Listen again. Which expressions did the speakers use to clarify what they said?

7 | SPEAKING PRACTICE

1. Work with a partner. Read the situations and discuss possible reasons why each situation is happening.

1. A large communications company has introduced free language and management classes for employees, but the employees aren't signing up for the classes.

   Possible reasons:

   <u>Maybe the classes aren't at convenient times.</u>

2. A company has introduced a computerized system of record-keeping, but most employees still use the old manual system.

   Possible reasons:

   _____

3. A very successful paper and stationery store moved to a new larger space, but fewer customers come to the store now.

   Possible reasons:

   _____

2. Make a list of questions that an anthropologist might ask in the above situations and what he or she might want to observe.

3. Change partners and choose one situation to role play. Student A: Act as the anthropologist who is trying to get information about what is happening and why. Student B: Act as a worker or customer. Use ideas from your lists and expressions to clarify as necessary. When you finish, change partners again and choose another situation to role play.

8 | TAKING SKILLS FURTHER

Listen to conversations outside of class. Notice when people clarify what they have said. What expressions do they use? Talk about your findings in the next class.

For additional listening practice on the topic of anthropology, go to the *Open Forum* Web site (www.oup.com/elt/openforum) and follow the links.

ABOUT THIS CHAPTER

Topic:	Money
Listening Texts:	Radio report about local currencies; informal lecture about the history of money
Listening Skill Focus:	Working out unknown vocabulary
Speaking Skill Focus:	Asking for further information
Vocabulary:	Words related to money
Pronunciation:	Intonation in lists

1 INTRODUCING THE TOPIC

1. Work with a partner. Read the quiz and discuss possible answers. (The answers are at the bottom of the page.)

What do you know about money?

You use your money every day, but how much do you really know about it? Take this quiz to find out more.

Which one of the following statements is false?

	True	False
1. Before money, people used shells, tools, and animal skins for trading.	☐	☐
2. Coins were first introduced around 600 B.C.	☐	☐
3. Only about 8 percent of the world's currency exists in cash.	☐	☐
4. The dollar is the only currency in the United States.	☐	☐
5. In the United States two-dollar banknotes are currently in circulation.	☐	☐

2. Read the answers to the quiz. Which fact surprises you the most?

Answers: 1. True, 2. True, 3. True. The rest of the world's currency is held in electronic bank accounts around the world, 4. False. Some towns and counties use local currencies as well as the dollar, 5. True. The two-dollar bill is no longer being printed, but it is still in circulation.

3. Match the words on the left with the definitions on the right. Then compare answers with a partner.

  _c_ 1. trading   **a.** piece of paper money

  ____ 2. coins   **b.** the system of money that is used in a particular place

  ____ 3. currency   **c.** exchanging goods and services between people

  ____ 4. banknote   **d.** being used between people, passed from one person to another

  ____ 5. in circulation   **e.** pieces of metal that are used as money

2 LISTENING PRACTICE

A Preparing to Listen

Work with a partner. Look at the picture. Discuss possible answers to the questions.

1. What is a local currency?
2. Why might some communities use a local currency?

B Listening for Main Ideas

 Listen to the radio report about a town that has issued its own currency. Then answer the questions in section A above.

C Listening for More Detail

Read the questions and answer the ones that you can. Then listen to the report again and complete your answers. Compare answers with a partner. Listen again if necessary.

1. What picture is on the Wilks banknote? _____

_____

2. How much is one hour worth? _____

_____

3. Where can the money be used? _____

_____

4. How much of the Wilks currency is in circulation? _____

_____

5. How many businesses accept the local currency? _____

_____

6. What do businesses do with the money they receive? _____

_____

7. How many other examples of local currencies are mentioned? _____

_____

8. What is written on the back of the Wilks bills? _____

_____

D Focus on the Listening Skill: Working Out Unknown Vocabulary

> **SPEAKING SKILL**
>
> If you do not know what a word or expression means, use these strategies to work out the meaning.
>
> - Pay attention to how the speaker uses the word in the sentence. Try to identify the part of speech (noun, adjective, verb, etc.).
> - Listen to see if the speaker defines the word. Sometimes a speaker explains the meaning of the word, or uses a simpler word right afterward.
> - Use the general meaning of the sentence and your background knowledge to help you work out the meaning.

1. **Read and listen to the extract from the radio report. Look at the example below to see how the meaning of *objective* was worked out.**

   Reporter: And what do the businesses do with the money? I mean, can they cash it in or . . . ?

   Moore: Well, they can cash it in, but that's not the objective! What we want to do is to keep the currency in the community. Employers use it to pay part of their employees' salaries. Or they pay for local services with it. So you see, it re-circulates. It goes back into the community that way.

   Objective probably means _____.
   - (a.) aim or goal
   - b. problem

   How did you know? *The next sentence says "What we want to do is . . ." What someone*

   wants to do is an aim or goal.

2. **Listen to the extract again. Then choose the correct meaning for *re-circulates* and explain the reason for your choice.**

   Re-circulates probably means _____.
   - a. to earn interest
   - b. to go back into a system and move around in it

   How did you know? _____

   _____

3. **For each item, listen to the extract and try to work out the meaning of the word in italics. Compare answers with a partner. Discuss the reasons for your choices.**

   1. *Legal tender* probably means _____.
      - a. money that can be used legally
      - b. equal to one dollar

   2. *Stimulate* probably means _____.
      - a. to make something famous or well-known
      - b. to make something more active or to encourage it

   3. *Issued* probably means _____.
      - a. produced
      - b. wanted

E Thinking and Speaking

Work with a partner. Discuss the questions.

1. How does using local currency help the community?

2. Can you think of disadvantages to using local currency?

3 | VOCABULARY: Words Related to Money

1. Read the paragraphs from a textbook. Then find a word in bold to match each definition below.

> If you want to be financially healthy, it's important to balance your income and your expenses. Income is the money that you earn from work or receive from other sources. For most people, their main income is their **salary.** Most people have to pay tax on their income (called **income tax**) to the government.
>
> Expenses are the things you have to pay for on a regular basis. Income tax is a type of expense. We all have to pay **bills** every month. For example, your expenses might include your **rent** or utility bills. Many people have to make **car payments** or repay **student loans.** People who own a home usually have a **mortgage** to repay. A mortgage is a home loan.
>
> It's quite easy to **borrow** money for large purchases. Banks and stores like to offer **credit** to consumers. That means that they will **lend** you money if you pay the money back later with an extra **interest** charge.
>
> It can be useful to have credit. It allows you to buy things now and pay for them later. But if you borrow too much money, it's easy to get into **debt.** Suddenly, you can find that you **owe** more than you can **pay back.**
>
> Your Money   23

1. Money that you make in a job: _____ <u>salary</u> _____

2. Money that you pay a landlord or landlady to live in a house or apartment:

   _____

3. Money that students borrow to go to college: _____

4. A loan to buy a house or apartment: _____

5. The opposite of *borrow*: _____

6. Extra money that you pay when you repay a loan: _____

7. To be in debt to another person: _____

8. Another way to say *repay*: _____

2. **Complete the paragraph with boldface words from page 46. Change the form of the words wherever necessary. Then compare answers with a partner.**

When I graduated college and started working full-time, I got my own apartment, bought a car, and felt very independent. But I had no idea how to manage my money. My income was lower than I expected, and I hadn't realized that I would have to pay so much (1) _____income tax_____ on my salary. Since I lived alone, I had to pay (2) _____ for the apartment by myself. I had bought a nice car, so I had to make car (3) _____, and I also had a student (4) _____ to repay. I didn't have enough money to pay all my (5) _____, so I started using (6) _____ cards. The (7) _____ charges on my cards were very high, so I got further into (8) _____. I soon realized that I was in trouble, and I had to make some hard choices. I got a roommate to help pay the rent. I sold the car and started taking the bus. Slowly, I (9) _____ all the money that I had (10) _____. Now that I've learned my lesson, I'm much more careful with money.

3. **Work in small groups. Discuss the questions.**

What advice would you give to each of the following people about money?
1. A teenager who has just started his/her first summer job
2. A student living away from home for the first time
3. A friend who has won $20,000 in a lottery

A | Preparing to Listen

You are going to listen to a lecture about the history of money. Work with a partner. Describe the pictures using some of the words below. Then discuss how each word might be connected to the topic.

| coins | grain | pound | trade | weigh |

B | Listening for Main Ideas

 Listen to the lecture. As you listen, check the four main topics that are discussed.

_____ A common currency

_____ Examples of a common currency

_____ How credit cards came about

_____ The first, coins, banks, and paper money

_____ The gold standard

_____ Investing in the stock market

C Listening for More Detail

🎧 Listen to the lecture again. As you listen, choose the correct answer to complete each statement. Then compare answers with a partner. Listen again if necessary.

1. It's not always convenient to trade by exchanging goods because _____.
   a. you can't always get what you want when you want it
   b. you can't always trust the other person

2. A common currency is something that _____.
   a. is made of gold or precious metal
   b. has value for everybody in a society

3. Beads, shells, tools, and grain were all _____.
   a. used as currency
   b. used for decoration

4. The English currency is called the pound because _____.
   a. it is very heavy
   b. grain was used as currency

5. The first coins appeared _____.
   a. around 600 B.C.
   b. after the first banks

6. The first banks were _____.
   a. places where people changed money
   b. places where people kept grain or gold

7. Banknotes were originally _____.
   a. made of gold
   b. receipts

8. The U.S. Government backed the dollar with real gold _____.
   a. after 1971
   b. until 1971

D Working Out Unknown Vocabulary

🎧 Listen to the extracts from the lecture. Listen for the words in italics. Choose the correct meaning for each word. Then compare answers with a partner.

1. *Barter* probably means _____.
   a. exchanging one item for another
   b. using a common currency

2. *Spoil* probably means _____.
   a. get stolen
   b. rot or go bad

3. A *spade* is probably _____.
   a. a type of knife
   b. a type of tool

4. A *depository* is probably ___.
   a. a type of warehouse
   b. a type of bank

5. *Came about* probably means ___.
   a. originated or started
   b. disappeared

E Thinking and Speaking

Work in small groups. Discuss the questions.

1. What did you learn from the lecture that you did not know before?

2. What did the lecturer mean when he explained that nothing backs our money in the United States except people's trust in it?

3. Have you ever experienced a situation where money lost its value? If so, describe the situation.

5 PRONUNCIATION: Intonation in Lists

FYI
Intonation is the way your voice goes up and down when you speak. Items in a list are usually spoken with rising intonation until the final item. The final item has falling intonation. This shows that the list has ended.

1. Listen to the sentences. Pay attention to the intonation. Rising intonation is marked like this: (↗) Falling intonation is marked like this: (↘)

   1. Some common currencies were beads, shells, tools, and grain.

   2. Coins were used in Ancient Greece, Turkey, and China.

   3. Money is used for trading, for paying fines, and for paying debts.

   4. My biggest expenses are rent, car payments, utility bills, and food.

   5. You can pay by cash, by check, or with a credit card.

2. **Work with a partner. Practice saying the sentences with appropriate intonation.**

6 | SPEAKING SKILLS: Asking for Further Information

SPEAKING SKILL

It's OK to ask for more information if you need it. Use expressions like the ones below to ask for more information about a subject.

> Can you tell me / us about . . . ?
> Could you tell us a little more about . . . ?
> I'd like to know more about . . .
> What about . . . ?
> Is that how / when / where (etc.) . . . ?

Listen to the extracts from the lecture. Which expressions do the students use to ask for more information?

7 | SPEAKING PRACTICE

1. Work in small groups. Think of some practical ways to save money on each of the items below. Write your suggestions in the chart. Then work with another group, compare your ideas, and add more suggestions.

1. rent	live with parents or share apartment with roommates
2. food	
3. heat, gas, and electricity	
4. telephone bills	
5. entertainment (music, movies)	

2. Work in small groups. Discuss the questions.

    1. Which ways of saving money are easy for you? Which are difficult?

    2. If someone gave you $10,000 right now, how would you spend it?

8 | TAKING SKILLS FURTHER

Outside of class, listen for the different ways that people ask for further information. What expressions do they use? Talk about your findings in the next class.

www For additional listening practice on the topic of money, go to the *Open Forum* Web site (www.oup.com/elt/openforum) and follow the links.

Topics:	Physical fitness; stress
Listening Texts:	Conversation about fidgeting and fitness; radio book review
Listening Skill Focus:	Identifying speculative language
Speaking Skill Focus:	Using expressions to show interest
Vocabulary:	Multi-word verbs (1)
Pronunciation:	Using intonation to show interest

1 INTRODUCING THE TOPIC

1. Work with a partner. Read the quiz and discuss possible answers. (The answers are at the bottom of the page.)

Health Quiz

How much do you know about staying healthy?

Decide whether each statement is **true** or **false**

1. Physical activity must be strenuous in order to get health benefits.

2. Doing housework at a moderate level can burn up to 300 calories per hour.

3. The amount of TV a child watches has no effect on his or her weight.

4. Eating a wide range of colors of fruit and vegetables is beneficial.

5. Having a pet can reduce stress levels and help you fight illness.

6. Thirty minutes of physical activity at least twice a week is recommended to stay healthy.

---

2. Compare answers with other students. What other recommendations do you know of to stay healthy?

Answers: 1. F, 2. T, 3. F, 4. T, 5. T, 6. T

2 | LISTENING PRACTICE

A Preparing to Listen

1. Work with a partner. Read the definition and the newspaper headline. Discuss what you think the newspaper article might be about.

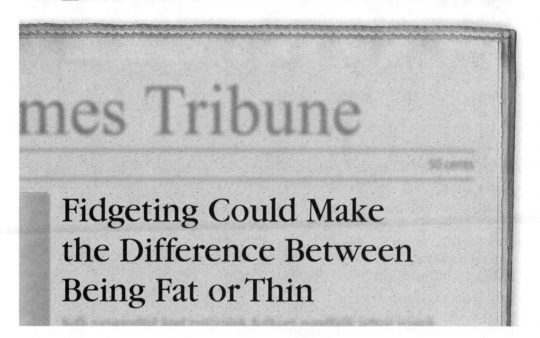

fidget *v:* to move around or play with something in a restless way because you are nervous, bored, etc.

Dictionary **93**

mes Tribune

Fidgeting Could Make the Difference Between Being Fat or Thin

2. Work in small groups and compare your ideas.

B Listening for Main Ideas

Listen to the conversation between two friends discussing a newspaper article. Then check the three main ideas discussed. (All the ideas are mentioned.) Compare answers with a partner.

_____ Fidgeting can help you be in better shape.

_____ Tapping your foot is an example of fidgeting.

_____ Researchers think people may be born with a tendency to move or not move a lot.

_____ The people in the study wore special sensors that measured movement.

_____ The sensors took measurements every half second.

C Listening for More Detail

 Listen to the conversation again. As you listen, choose the correct answer for each item. Then compare answers with a partner. Listen again if necessary.

1. The research study was done at a clinic in _____.
   a. Michigan
   b. Missouri
   c. Minnesota

2. According to the study, how much more time do overweight people spend sitting still?
   a. at least an hour
   b. at least two hours
   c. at least three hours

3. The extra activity of a thinner person might make a difference in weight of _____.
   a. about 10 to 30 pounds per year
   b. about 10 pounds per year
   c. about 30 pounds per year

4. The fact that some people are born with a tendency to fidget is not discouraging to the lead researcher because _____.
   a. a lot of people can train to run 10 miles
   b. people can change this tendency
   c. small movements and activities can contribute to fitness

5. The people in the study wore the clothes with sensors _____.
   a. 10 hours a day for 20 days
   b. 24 hours a day for 10 days
   c. 24 hours a day for 20 days

6. Compared to overweight people, thin people moved _____.
   a. 150 minutes more
   b. 50 minutes more
   c. 100 minutes more

D Focus on the Listening Skill: Identifying Speculative Language

> **LISTENING SKILL**
>
> When you listen to a news report or to the results of a scientific study, it is important to tell the difference between information the speaker gives as fact and information that is speculative. Speculative information is information that might not be accurate. When presenting speculative information, speakers often use language like the words below.

possibly	it could be
apparently	I think
it might be	it's possible that

 1. Listen to the sentences from the conversation. Decide whether each piece of information is fact or whether it is speculative. Circle the correct answer.

1.   fact   speculative

2.   fact   speculative

3.   fact   speculative

4.   fact   speculative

5.   fact   speculative

6.   fact   speculative

2. Listen to the sentences again. Work with a partner. Discuss which words helped you decide if the information is factual or speculative.

E Thinking and Speaking

Work with a partner. Summarize what the researchers did and what they found. Then discuss the questions.

1. In what ways is this research on physical fitness useful?

2. What other kinds of small changes could people make in their daily activities to help them keep fit?

3 | VOCABULARY: Multi-Word Verbs (1)

FYI

Multi-word verbs are made up of a verb (*get, put, turn*) and one or more particles (*on, off, up*). Many multi-word verbs are separable. This means that a noun object can appear either before a particle or after it.
Example:
Throw away <u>the remote</u>. (correct)
Throw <u>the remote</u> away. (correct)

However, with these types of multi-word verbs, when the object is a pronoun (*it, them, her*), it must come before the particle.
Example:
Throw away it. (incorrect)
Throw <u>it</u> away. (correct)

Other common multi-word verbs that follow this pattern are *turn on, turn off, put on,* and *pick up.*

1. **Read the paragraph. Circle the multi-word verbs. One is done for you. There are nine more.**

   Researchers have new information about staying in shape. Almost any little movement could help you stay fit and (take off) some unwanted pounds. You don't have to go out and run 10 miles! If you're on the sofa, just get up. That's right, stand up and stretch. If you do this several times a day, it will help. If you feel more ambitious, turn off the TV, put on your shoes and go out for a walk. Then when you sit down to watch TV again, don't pick up the remote. In fact, throw it away. That way you have to move to watch TV.

2. **Read the sentences below. Re-write them, changing the underlined words to pronouns.**

   1. Could you please turn on <u>the radio</u>?

      Could you please turn it on?

   2. She picked up <u>the papers</u>.

      _____

   3. He put on <u>his hat</u> before he went out.

      _____

   4. Throw away <u>the milk</u>. It's gone bad.

      _____

   5. Don't forget to turn off <u>the lights</u> when you leave.

      _____

6. Take off <u>your shoes</u> when you come into the house, please.

_____

3. Write three to five sentences about what you usually do before you leave your home or what you do when you return home. Use as many multi-word verbs as you can. Then compare your sentences in a small group.

4 | LISTENING PRACTICE

A Preparing to Listen

1. You are going to listen to a review of a book called *Why Zebras Don't Get Ulcers*. Look at the picture of the book. What do you think it is about? What are ulcers?

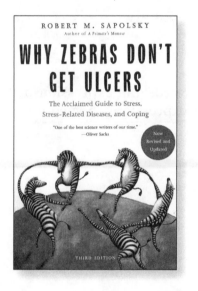

2. What are some of the effects of stress on a person's health?

B Listening for Main Ideas

 Listen to the book review. Choose the correct ending for the summary of the book.

In his book, Robert Sapolsky says _____.
   a. Human stress is more like zebra stress
   b. Human stress is more like baboon stress

C Listening for More Detail

 Listen to the review again. As you listen, complete the statements. Then compare answers with a partner. Listen again if necessary.

1. Robert Sapolsky came to conclusions about human stress after _____

_____

2. Stress that zebras might feel is _____

   _____

3. Baboons have more free time because _____

   _____

4. Some typical causes of stress in humans mentioned are _____

   _____

5. Long-term stress in humans causes problems because _____

   _____

6. To deal with stress, Robert Sapolsky suggests _____

   _____

D Working Out Unknown Vocabulary

Listen to the extracts from the review. Listen for the words and expressions in italics. Choose the correct meaning for each word or expression. Then compare answers with a partner.

1. *Made parallels to* probably means _____.
   a. made comparisons or found similarities
   b. found differences

2. *Searching for* probably means _____.
   a. preparing food to eat
   b. looking for or trying to find

3. *Chronic stress* probably means _____.
   a. stress that only lasts a short time
   b. stress that lasts a long time

4. *Entertaining* probably means _____.
   a. something that is interesting and amusing
   b. something that gives lots of information

E Thinking and Speaking

Work in small groups. Discuss the questions.

1. Do you agree with the parallels Robert Sapolsky makes between stress in humans and stress in zebras and baboons? Why or why not?

2. Think back to your answers in section A (page 57). Can you add or change anything to those answers after listening?

5 | PRONUNCIATION: Using Intonation to Show Interest

 Intonation is the way your voice goes up and down when you speak. It can help show interest and emotion. Your voice is likely to go up and down more when you are interested and enthusiastic. If your intonation does not change enough, you may seem bored or uninterested.

1. Listen to the extracts from the book review. Pay attention to Kellie's intonation when she responds to Gordon.

2. Listen again to one of Kellie's responses. Which version shows interest with the intonation? Which sounds less interested?

3. Work in pairs. Practice the two short dialogues below. Make sure you use changes in intonation to show interest.

   A: I have a great new idea to reduce stress.

   B: Really? What is it?

   A: Would you like to go to the gym with me?

   B: Sure! When are you going?

6 | SPEAKING SKILLS: Using Expressions to Show Interest

SPEAKING SKILL

You can use the expressions in the list below to show interest in a topic. Remember to say these expressions with appropriate intonation. Note that asking questions is also a way to show interest.

Really?
Hmm.
I see.
Interesting!
That sounds interesting.
I didn't know that.
That's a good idea.

1. Listen to the conversation. What are the people talking about?

2. Listen again. Which expressions do the speakers use to show interest?

7 | SPEAKING PRACTICE

1. Work with a partner. Look at the list of activities in the box below and answer the questions.

cooking	gardening	reading the newspaper	watching a movie
doing laundry	listening to music	surfing the Internet	watching sports
driving	paying bills	talking with friends	watching TV
exercising	playing sports	washing dishes	working

1. Which of these activities make you feel less stressed? Which ones make you feel more stressed? Why do these activities have this effect on your stress level?

2. Are there any other activities that affect your stress level?

3. What are the two best things for you to do to reduce stress?

2. Compare your answers in small groups. How similar or different are the activities that cause stress for you? How similar or different are the ones that reduce stress for you?

8 | TAKING SKILLS FURTHER

In your conversations outside of class, notice what expressions people use to show interest. Pay attention to how they use intonation to show interest as well. Talk about what you noticed in the next class.

 For additional listening practice on the topic of fitness and stress, go to the *Open Forum* Web site (www.oup.com/elt/openforum) and follow the links.

CHAPTER 8 Social Studies

ABOUT THIS CHAPTER

Topics:	Community and social involvement
Listening Texts:	Interview with a sociologist; on-the-street interviews about community involvement
Listening Skill Focus:	Listening for specific information
Speaking Skill Focus:	Elaborating
Vocabulary:	Describing trends
Pronunciation:	Unstressed object pronouns

1 INTRODUCING THE TOPIC

1. Most people belong to more than one community. For example, our families are one community; the people at work or at school are another. Read the list of communities below and add any others that you can think of.

Family   Sports team

Friends   _____

Co-workers or classmates   _____

Neighbors or local community   _____

Online friends   _____

2. Work in small groups. Discuss the questions below.

   1. Which of the communities listed above are you part of?

   2. Which communities are most important for you? Which ones are least important?

   3. Do you think it is important to be involved in one or more communities? Why or why not?

2 | LISTENING PRACTICE

A Preparing to Listen

Look at the statements. Circle the word that you think makes each statement true. Then compare answers with a partner. Discuss the reasons for your choices.

1. People in the United States are **more / less** involved in their communities than they were 50 years ago.

2. People are **more / less** interested in politics than they used to be.

3. Americans visit with friends and family **more / less** than they used to.

B Listening for Main Ideas

 Listen to an interview with a sociologist. As you listen, check your answers to the items above.

C Listening for More Detail

 Listen to the interview again. As you listen, choose the correct answer to each question. Then compare answers with a partner. Listen again if necessary.

1. Which example of involvement in the local community is NOT mentioned?
   a. membership in the PTA
   b. attending a church, synagogue, or mosque
   c. attending meetings about local issues

2. Which example of interest in the political process is NOT mentioned?
   a. reading the newspaper
   b. voting in elections
   c. working on political campaigns

3. Which example of informal social activity is NOT mentioned?
   a. going out to restaurants
   b. having friends to dinner
   c. visiting neighbors

4. Which point is NOT made about social involvement?
   a. Places where there is a lot of social involvement have less crime.
   b. People who are socially connected are happier and healthier.
   c. People who are socially connected work harder and earn more.

5. Which suggestion is NOT made?
   a. People should get more involved in local elections.
   b. People should volunteer more.
   c. People should get to know their neighbors.

D Focus on the Listening Skill: Listening for Specific Information

> **LISTENING SKILL**
>
> When there is a lot of detailed information in a lecture or a talk, it can be hard to identify the information you want to hear. Practice listening for the specific information that you want, without being distracted by other details.

Look through the questions to identify the information you need. Then listen to part of the interview again and choose the correct answer for each question. Listen again if necessary.

1. When was PTA membership very high?
   a. in the 1950s
   b. in the 1960s
   c. in 1995

2. What has gone down by 60 percent?
   a. bus service
   b. crime in certain neighborhoods
   c. the number of people who attend public meetings

3. What percentage of younger Americans read a newspaper every day?
   a. 25 percent
   b. 80 percent
   c. 85 percent

4. In 1900, what percentage of voters turned out to vote?
   a. 100 percent
   b. 85 percent
   c. less than 50 percent

5. When did people "have a better social life"?
   a. in the 1950s
   b. in the 1960s
   c. in 1995

E Thinking and Speaking

Work with a partner. Explain in your own words what was said in the interview about each of the following topics. Then give your opinion about each topic.

- community involvement in the past and the present

- informal social connections in the past and the present

- the importance of social involvement in a community

3 VOCABULARY: Describing Trends

1. Look at the graph and read the description. Pay attention to the words and expressions in bold.

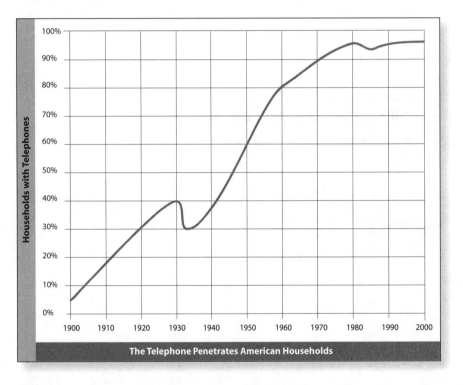

The Telephone Penetrates American Households

The percentage of households with a telephone **increased steadily** in the beginning of the 20th century, reaching a **peak** of **approximately** 40 percent in 1930. In 1933, the percentage **fell** to about 30 percent as a result of the Depression. However, between 1933 and 1970 there was again a steady **rise** in the number of households with telephones. The figure finally **leveled off** at about 94 percent between 1980 and 2000.

2. **Match a word in bold from the description on page 64 with the correct definition below.**

Word	Definition
<u>increased</u>	went up or rose
_____	went down or decreased
_____	an increase
_____	about or around
_____	in an even or regular way
_____	the highest point
_____	reached and stayed at the same level

3. **Look at the graph. Then circle the correct words to complete the description. Compare answers with a partner.**

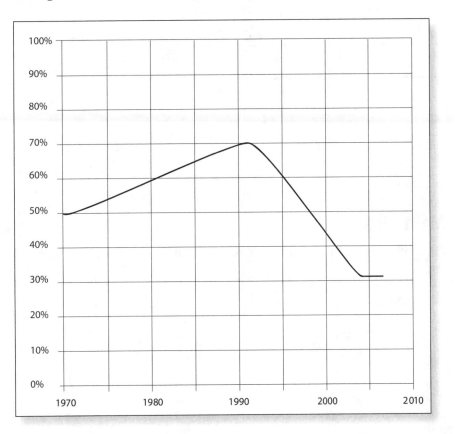

The percentage (1) increased / decreased (2) suddenly / steadily between 1970

and 1990, (3) reaching a peak / leveling off of 70 percent in 1992. After that,

the figure (4) rose / fell steeply, finally (5) reaching a peak / leveling off at

(6) approximately / exactly 30 percent in 2004.

4. **Work with a partner. Choose one of the graphs and describe it without looking at the text. Use the words from exercise 2.**

A Preparing to Listen

Some students are doing a survey on social involvement. Here are some of the questions in the survey.

> How many of your neighbors' first names do you know?
> How often do you attend parades or festivals (in one year)?
> Do you volunteer?
> Do you sign petitions?

Think of some other questions that the students might ask people in order to judge how involved they are in their communities.

_____

_____

_____

_____

_____

_____

_____

_____

B Listening for Main Ideas

Listen to the interviews. Check the two types of social involvement that are NOT discussed.

_____ knowing your neighbors

_____ attending a church, mosque, or synagogue

_____ attending local events

_____ reading or listening to the news

_____ volunteering

_____ getting together with friends and family

C Listening for More Detail

Listen again and make notes in the interviewer's chart.

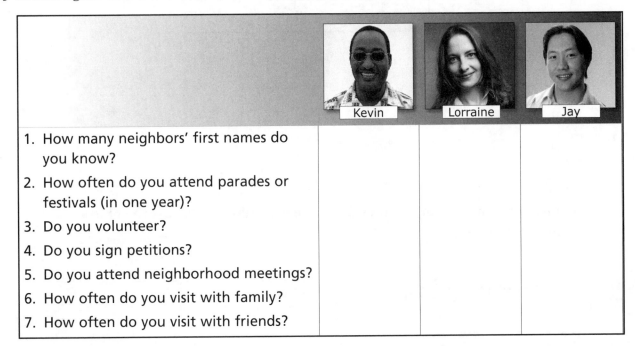

	Kevin	Lorraine	Jay
1. How many neighbors' first names do you know?			
2. How often do you attend parades or festivals (in one year)?			
3. Do you volunteer?			
4. Do you sign petitions?			
5. Do you attend neighborhood meetings?			
6. How often do you visit with family?			
7. How often do you visit with friends?			

D Thinking and Speaking

Work in pairs or small groups. Discuss the questions.

1. Think about how the three people answered the questions. Are you surprised by anything that they said?

2. How useful are these questions as a way to measure social involvement? Give reasons for your answers.

5 PRONUNCIATION: Unstressed Object Pronouns

Object pronouns (*me, you, him, her, it, us,* and *them*) are usually unstressed in spoken English. They can be difficult to hear accurately because they are unstressed. Pay attention to the context in which these different words occur. This can help you identify which word is being used.

1. Read and listen to the extract from one of the interviews. Choose the correct pronoun to complete the sentence. How did you know which pronoun was correct?

Well my parents and my brothers all live a long way away, so we only get to

see _____ once a year.

a. him

b. her

c. them

🎧 2. Now listen to five more extracts. For each one, write the object pronoun that you hear. Choose from the list.

him	her	them	you	it

Extract 1. _____

Extract 2. _____

Extract 3. _____

Extract 4. _____

Extract 5. _____

🎧 3. Listen again. Repeat each sentence. Be careful not to stress the object pronouns.

6 SPEAKING SKILLS: Elaborating

SPEAKING SKILL

When someone asks you a question, it can sound impolite to reply with just *yes, no,* or another one-word answer. Try to say a little more. This makes you sound friendly and helps to keep the conversation going.

🎧 1. Listen to how the people respond to the questions. Do they say only *yes* or *no,* or do they say more? What is the effect?

2. Look at the questions from the survey. Answer each question. Then think of ways to elaborate on the answers. Practice asking and answering the questions with a partner.

1. How often do you attend parades or festivals? _____

_____

2. Do you volunteer? _____

_____

3. How often do you visit with family? _____

_____

4. How often do you visit with friends? _____

_____

7 | SPEAKING PRACTICE

1. Work with a partner. Read the situations below. For each situation, decide how you would let people know about the problem that is described and how you might persuade others to join you.

   Situation 1

   A natural disaster has happened elsewhere in the world. Nobody at your school or university has organized a way of collecting donations to help the victims. What would be the best way to collect the most possible donations?

   Situation 2

   There is a lot of trash and litter in a public park near where you live. The city authorities have told you that they do not have the money to maintain the park. You would like to get some neighbors together to help clean up the park. How could you do that?

   Situation 3

   You have a large dog that needs to be walked daily. You do not know many people in your neighborhood, but many people have dogs—and you would like to have company while you walk your dog. What could you do?

2. Work in small groups. Take turns describing what you would do in each situation above. Which plan do you think would be most successful in each case?

8 | TAKING SKILLS FURTHER

Next time you listen to the news on TV or on the radio, identify a topic on the news that you would like to know more about. Then think of some specific information that you would like to hear, and practice listening specifically for it. Talk about your experience in the next class.

For additional listening practice on the topic of community involvement, go to the *Open Forum* Web site (www.oup.com/elt/openforum) and follow the links.

ABOUT THIS CHAPTER

Topics:	Weather and water
Listening Texts:	News program about running in the rain; lecture on water projects around the world
Listening Skill Focus:	Identifying sequencers
Speaking Skill Focus:	Saying percentages and fractions
Vocabulary:	Collocations with *make* and *do*
Pronunciation:	Linking

1 INTRODUCING THE TOPIC

1. Read the weather forecast. Then work with a partner and discuss the questions.

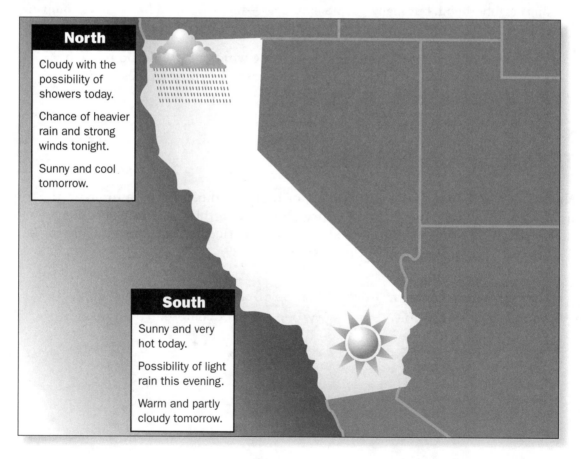

North

Cloudy with the possibility of showers today.

Chance of heavier rain and strong winds tonight.

Sunny and cool tomorrow.

South

Sunny and very hot today.

Possibility of light rain this evening.

Warm and partly cloudy tomorrow.

1. How reliable are weather forecasts? Why do you think this is?
2. What kind of weather do you prefer? Why?

2. Work with a partner. Write a short description of the weather in your area today. Then compare your description with other students. How similar or different are your descriptions?

2 | LISTENING PRACTICE

A Preparing to Listen

1. Work with a partner. Read the statement and the possible answers below. Discuss which answer you think is correct. Give reasons for your answer.

If it starts to rain and you don't have an umbrella, _____.
   a. you will stay drier if you run to shelter
   b. you will stay drier if you walk to shelter
   c. it doesn't matter if you walk or run

2. Compare answers as a class. What is the most popular answer?

B Listening for Main Ideas

 Listen to the news report. Then check your answer from section A above. Were you correct?

C Listening for More Detail

 Listen to the report again. Make notes to complete each statement. Compare notes with a partner. Listen again if necessary.

1. It seems like you'll get wetter if you walk in the rain because _____

   _____.

2. You might get wetter when you run because the rain _____

   _____.

3. Wind could make a difference because _____

   _____.

4. If you run in a light rain without wind, _____

   _____.

5. If you run in a heavy rain with a lot of wind, _____

   _____.

6. Two scientists found this difference by _____

   _____.

D Focus on the Listening Skill: Identifying Sequencers

> **LISTENING SKILL**
>
> When speakers are describing or explaining events, they sometimes use sequencing expressions such as *First . . .* , *Next . . .* , or *Then . . . .* Noticing these expressions can help you understand the description or explanation more easily.

1. Listen to the extract from the news report. One of the newscasters is describing the experiment that the scientists did. As you listen, number the events in the correct order. The first one has been done for you.

_____ They waited for a rainstorm.

_____ Other people were interested in the results.

__1__ They decided to do an experiment.

_____ They weighed their clothes to find out how much water was absorbed.

_____ They measured a track outside their office.

_____ One man walked around the track, and one man ran around it.

_____ They bought identical clothes.

2. Listen to the extract again. Check the sequencing expressions that the newscaster uses.

_____ First,

_____ Then,

_____ After that,

_____ After (they finished),

_____ In the end,

_____ Finally,

E Thinking and Speaking

Work in small groups. Discuss the questions.

1. Do you think this research on running in the rain is useful? If so, in what ways?

2. What other research on weather do you know of?

3. In what ways can weather research help us in our daily lives?

3 | VOCABULARY: Collocations with *Make* and *Do*

1. **Read the sentences and circle *make* and *do*. Then underline the noun phrase that follows *make* or *do*.**

   I think it <u>makes sense </u>to run in the rain.

   How did they <u>do the research? </u>

   Wind <u>makes a difference</u> in the calculation.

   Two scientists in North Carolina decided <u>to do an experiment.</u>

   FYI We often use *make* with things that we create, build, or earn. We often use *do* with jobs or tasks.

2. **Look at the following list of items and decide whether each one is used with *make* or *do*. Add each expression to the correct column. Then listen and check your answers.**

business	a job	a meal	a profit
a decision	a list	a mistake	the shopping
housework	a living	money	someone a favor

make	do

3. **Read the sentences below. Circle the correct verb, *make* or *do*. Compare your answers with a partner.**

   1. The scientists don't want to **make / do** a mistake in their experiment.

   2. It doesn't **make / do** sense to carry an umbrella on a sunny day.

   3. We need to **make / do** a decision soon. Everyone is waiting.

   4. My sister **makes / does** research for an organization that studies weather patterns.

   5. Let's **make / do** a list of the things we need before we go shopping.

   6. Could you **make / do** me a favor and bring me my umbrella? I think it's going to rain.

7. Does it **make / do** a difference whether I run or walk in the rain?

8. When the company **makes / does** a profit, the employees get a bonus at the end of the year.

4 LISTENING PRACTICE

A Preparing to Listen

1. Work with a partner. Look at the pictures. Then make a list of the different ways that water affects our lives. Use the examples to get started.

We have to drink water.

Plants and crops need water to grow.

_____

_____

_____

_____

2. Work in small groups and compare your lists. As a group, decide what the three most important uses of water are.

B Listening for Main Ideas

Listen to the lecture from a conference on global water issues. Number the water projects below in the order they are mentioned.

_____ Rain barrels to collect water for gardens

_____ Residents who built a water system for their town

_____ Large ponds that use algae to clean waste water

C Listening for More Detail

Listen to the lecture again. Write *T* for true or *F* for false for each statement. Compare your answers with a partner and correct the false statements. Listen again if necessary.

_____ 1. They had an old water system in the town of San Elizario.

_____ 2. A typical family had a bucket of water for each member of the family.

_____ 3. The water authorities asked the people of the town to help build the water system.

_____ 4. The townspeople learned as they did the work.

_____ 5. Other people now want to learn how to do a similar project in their own towns.

_____ 6. The Calcutta Wetlands are in the center of Calcutta.

_____ 7. The water in the ponds is clean enough to drink.

_____ 8. The pond water is cleaned by algae.

_____ 9. The project in Vancouver is designed to provide water for people's gardens.

_____ 10. The Vancouver project is important because Vancouver doesn't get much rain.

D Working Out Unknown Vocabulary

Listen to the extracts from the lecture. Listen for the words in italics. Choose the correct meaning for each word. Compare answers with a partner.

1. *Buckets* are probably _____.
   a. containers for carrying water and other liquids
   b. containers for cooking

2. *Installed* probably means _____.
   a. fixed or repaired something
   b. put in place so something is ready to be used

3. *To set up* something probably means _____.
   a. to learn how to build something
   b. to start, build, or establish something

4. *Waste* is probably _____.
   a. material or food before people have used it
   b. material or food that is thrown away

5. *To irrigate* probably means _____.
   a. to put water on crops and plants
   b. to put new plants in the ground

E Thinking and Speaking

Work with a partner. Discuss the questions.

1. Which project mentioned in the presentation do you think is most helpful? Describe the project to your partner in your own words, and say why you think it is helpful.

2. Do you know of any other projects related to water? If so, describe them to your partner.

3. Do people in your community conserve water? If so, in what ways? If not, should they? Why or why not?

5 PRONUNCIATION: Linking

FYI

When a word that ends in a consonant sound is followed by a word beginning with a vowel sound, speakers often link the words by running them together without a break between. This is a natural feature of spoken language, but sometimes it is difficult to hear the linked words correctly.

1. **Read and listen to the sentences. Notice how the words ending in consonants are linked to the words beginning with vowels.**

   It's a sunny day.

   It rains a lot in the city.

   Grab an umbrella.

2. **Read the sentences. Draw linking marks where you think words ending in a consonant sound will link to words beginning with a vowel sound. Then listen and check your predictions.**

1. She has overseen many projects around the world.

2. Vancouver is a city that gets a lot of rain.

3. Calcutta is in India.

4. I think it's an important issue

3. **Practice saying the sentences above with natural linking.**

6 | SPEAKING SKILLS: Saying Percentages and Fractions

SPEAKING SKILL

It can be difficult to say certain kinds of numerical expressions, such as percentages and fractions. Look at the boxes below for some examples of numerical expressions and how to say them.

Percentages	
97.5%	ninety-seven point five percent
30%	thirty percent
2.5%	two point five percent
0.57%	point five seven percent
Fractions	
1/2	half
1/3	one third OR a third
1/4	one fourth, a fourth, OR a quarter
1/8	one eighth OR an eighth

1. **Listen to the lecturer give some statistics about water. What percentage of the world's fresh water is in lakes and rivers?**

2. **Listen again. Write the numerical expression(s) you hear for each sentence.**

1. ___97.5%___ of the world's water supply is saltwater.

2. _____ of the world's water supply is fresh water.

3. Almost _____, or _____, of freshwater is ice in glaciers.

4. _____, almost _____, of freshwater is in groundwater.

3. **Work with a partner. Practice saying the sentences above.**

7 SPEAKING PRACTICE

1. Work with a partner. Read the information in the charts about water supply and use. Then discuss the questions.

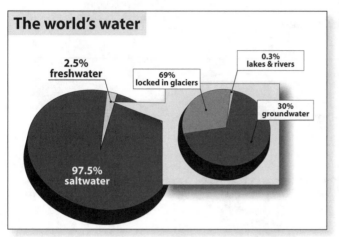

The world's water

2.5% freshwater

69% locked in glaciers

0.3% lakes & rivers

30% groundwater

97.5% saltwater

The amount of water on Earth is fixed. Very little of the earth's water is easily accessible freshwater in lakes and rivers.

Global water use

8% domestic

22% industry

70% agriculture

Global water use has tripled since 1950 and has been increasing faster than the world's population. Agriculture uses the most water - it takes at least 2,000 liters to produce enough food for one person for one day.

1. What does it mean that "the amount of water on Earth is fixed"?
2. How easy or difficult is it to access fresh water? Why?
3. For what purpose is the most water used?
4. Is global water use going up, staying the same, or going down? What are some possible effects of this?

2. Work in small groups and discuss your answers. What are some of the problems shown in these charts? What are some possible solutions?

8 TAKING SKILLS FURTHER

When you listen to people speaking outside of class, listen for sequencers. Do you hear the ones that you studied in this chapter or different ones? Talk about your findings in the next class.

For additional listening practice on the topic of rain and water, go to the *Open Forum* Web site (www.oup.com/elt/openforum) and follow the links.

Topics:	Explorers; Ellis Island
Listening Texts:	Conversation about the discovery of America; student presentation on Ellis Island
Listening Skill Focus:	Summarizing
Speaking Skill Focus:	Giving presentations
Vocabulary:	Multi-word verbs (2)
Pronunciation:	Unstressed and contracted auxiliary verbs

1 INTRODUCING THE TOPIC

1. Look at the map. Find the following places:

The Bering Strait	Iceland
China	Newfoundland
Greenland	The Pacific Ocean

2. Work in small groups. Discuss possible answers to the questions.

1. Where did the original Native Americans come from?

2. Where did the first explorers to North America come from? Where did they land?

2 | LISTENING PRACTICE

A Preparing to Listen

Read the descriptions of the explorers. Then work in small groups and answer the questions.

Born in Genoa, Italy, Christopher Columbus reached the Bahamas in 1492 while trying to find a westward route to the Orient.

The Viking Leif Erikson, son of Eric the Red, was the first European colonizer of Greenland in the 10th century.

Zheng He was a Chinese scholar, diplomat, and warrior who commanded the seas in the 15th century with a fleet of treasure ships.

1. Which two of the explorers lived at about the same time?

2. How much do you know about these explorers?

3. What other explorers do you know about?

B Listening for Main Ideas

Listen to the conversation between Aidan and Sandra. Number the people in the order that they are discussed.

_____ The first people to come to North America

_____ Leif Erikson

_____ Christopher Columbus

_____ Zheng He

C Listening for More Detail

Listen to the conversation again. As you listen, write *T* for true or *F* for false for each item. Compare answers with a partner. Correct the false statements.

_____ 1. Sandra is studying for a history test.

_____ 2. The first people to come to America came from South America.

_____ 3. There is evidence that the Vikings reached Newfoundland.

_____ 4. At the time of the Vikings, many Western Europeans believed that there was land in the West.

_____ 5. Zheng He lived around 1500.

_____ 6. Zheng He's ships and fleet were larger and more sophisticated than those of the Europeans.

_____ 7. Zheng He opened up trade between the Chinese and people in other countries.

_____ 8. It is certain that Zheng He reached America.

D Focus on the Listening Skill: Summarizing

> **LISTENING SKILL**
>
> Summarizing is taking the main points of what you hear and restating them in one or two sentences. Use summarizing to check that you have understood the main points in a presentation or a lecture. In a talk about a person or people, one way to summarize is to answer the questions: _Who is this about?_ and _What is said about the person or people?_

1. Listen to the extract from the presentation. Then choose the correct answers to the questions.

   1. Who is this about?
      a. Leif Erikson
      b. The Vikings

   2. What is said about the person or people?
      a. He/They colonized Norway.
      b. He/They reached Newfoundland.

   3. Now choose the best summary of Sandra's main point in this part of the presentation.
      a. Leif Erickson was a Viking.
      b. Newfoundland is close to Greenland.
      c. Leif Erickson sailed to Newfoundland.

2. Listen to another extract from the presentation. Then answer the questions.

   1. Who is this about? _____

   2. What is said about the person or people? _____

   _____

   3. Now write a summary of Sandra's main point in this part of the presentation.

   _____

   _____

E Thinking and Speaking

Work in pairs or small groups. Discuss the questions.

1. What are the different reasons why explorers came to the New World? Why do people come to the "New World" nowadays?

2. Why do you think some explorers are better known today than others?

---

3 VOCABULARY: Multi-Word Verbs (2)

 Many multi-word verbs can be expressed as a single verb. For example, another way to say *go out* is *leave*. Multi-word verbs are more common in speech and in informal conversation. Single verbs are more common in writing and more formal speech.

1. Underline the multi-word verb in each sentence. Then match each multi-word verb with a verb on the right that has a similar meaning.

_e_ 1. In 1492, Columbus <u>set out</u> on a voyage from Spain.	a. was discovered
____ 2. He thought he had reached India, but it turned out to be the Bahamas.	b. met
____ 3. The original Native Americans came in from the North.	c. entered
____ 4. Some people believe that Zheng He got to the American continent.	d. discovered
____ 5. Leif Erikson didn't stay in Newfoundland. He went back to Greenland.	e. left
____ 6. The first settlers went through a lot of hardships in the early years.	f. reached
____ 7. The students got together to prepare their presentation.	g. researched
____ 8. Sandra wanted more information about exploration, so she looked it up online.	h. returned
____ 9. Sandra found out that other explorers had reached the New World.	i. reviewed
____ 10. She went over her presentation with Aidan.	j. experienced

2. Only one of the multi-word verbs above is separable (the object can come between the verb and the particle). Which one is it? Read the sentences again and find it.

3. Complete the sentences with the correct forms of the multi-word verbs from exercise 1.

Last summer a group of us climbed to the top of Mount Wood. We planned the trip carefully. Drew (1) _____looked up_____ the area online and (2) _____ that there was a hut at the top of the mountain where we could stay. We (3) _____ a few weeks beforehand to discuss the trip and make plans. We (4) _____ the route several times, so that everybody would know the way. Finally the day came. We (5) _____ happily and with enough food for several days. Unfortunately, Debbie sprained her ankle on the first day and had to (6) _____ home, but other than that, it was an unforgettable trip. We expected the weather to be cold, but it (7) _____ to be bright and sunny every day. After three days, we (8) _____ the top of the mountain. The view was incredible!

4 LISTENING PRACTICE

A Preparing to Listen

Work in small groups. Look at the photograph taken at Ellis Island. Discuss the questions.

1. What do you know about Ellis Island?
2. What do you think is happening in the picture?

B Listening for Main Ideas

 Listen to a presentation about Ellis Island and number the topics in the order that they are mentioned.

_____ The "kissing post"

_____ The dining hall

_____ Researching your family background

_____ Arriving at Ellis Island

_____ The inspections

C Listening for More Detail

 Try to make some notes about each topic from the presentation. Then listen to the presentation again and add more details to your notes. Compare notes with a partner. Listen again if necessary.

Topic	Notes
1. Possessions that people brought to America	
2. The first meal	
3. How and why some people were held back	
4. The Great Hall	
5. The "kissing post"	
6. How Melissa's aunt found out about her grandfather	

D Working Out Unknown Vocabulary

 Listen to the extracts from the presentation. Listen for the words in italics. Choose the correct meaning for each word. Then compare answers with a partner.

1. The _docks_ are probably _____.
   a. a part of a ship
   b. a place where people can get on or off a ship

2. _Vines_ are probably _____.
   a. plants that grow grapes
   b. tools for gardening or planting

3. *Detained* probably means _____.
   a. stopped or prevented from leaving
   b. entertained

4. A *fiddle* is probably _____.
   a. a kind of game
   b. a musical instrument

5. A *relative* is probably _____.
   a. a member of the same family
   b. a small town

E Thinking and Speaking

Work in small groups. Discuss the questions.

1. How has the process of immigration changed since the days when people arrived at Ellis Island by boat?

2. Why do you think people like to research their family background?

3. How much do you know about your own family background? Would you like to know more?

5 PRONUNCIATION: Unstressed and Contracted Auxiliary Verbs

FYI Auxiliary verbs such as *was, were, can,* and *would* are often unstressed or contracted in spoken English. They can be difficult to hear accurately. Practice identifying contracted and unstressed auxiliary verbs as much as possible.

 1. **Listen to the extracts from the presentation. Fill in the missing auxiliary verbs.**

1. Our presentation is about Ellis Island. We went there last week and took a tour, and we _____'re_____ going to describe some of the things that we found out. First, Grace and I _____ talk about the process . . .

2. When they finally landed at Ellis Island, they _____ put on all the clothes they owned, because they _____ allowed to bring in only one bag with their possessions from the old country.

3. They _____ crowded together, and it was often very hot and very loud. You _____ imagine . . .

4. He died before I _____ born, but apparently he was a great musician. He _____ play the fiddle and sing at family events. Well, Joan knew that he _____ come from Cork, in Ireland . . .

2. Listen and repeat the sentences. Be careful not to stress the auxiliary verbs.

1. They were crowded together.
2. I can imagine.
3. He was born in Ireland.
4. He would play the fiddle.
5. He had come from Cork.

6 SPEAKING SKILLS: Giving Presentations

SPEAKING SKILL

It's important to prepare well for presentations. This will make your presentation clearer, and will help you feel more relaxed and confident when you present.

1. Work with a partner. Discuss the questions.

1. How do you feel about speaking in public? For example, how do you feel about giving presentations or reports in class?
2. What do you think is the best way to prepare for public speaking?

2. Read the strategies for giving presentations. Add one or two more strategies. Then compare your answers in small groups.

1. Don't try to say too much. Limit your presentation to a few main points.
2. Write your outline on index cards that are easy to refer to.
3. Talk through the presentation with a friend beforehand, or rehearse it by yourself.
4. Speak clearly during the presentation. Don't rush. Pause at changes of topic.
5. Look at the audience as much as you can. Make eye contact with different people in the audience.

6. _____

7. _____

7 | SPEAKING PRACTICE

1. Choose one of the following topics (or use your own idea) and prepare a short presentation. First, write down as many ideas about the topic as you can think of.

    Topics:

    Adapting to a different culture

    A story about one of my ancestors or relatives

    My family history

    A historical event that affected my life

2. Put the ideas in order. Prepare an outline of your presentation on a notebook page or on index cards.

3. Talk through your presentation with a partner.

4. Give your presentation in front of the class. Use some of the strategies that you discussed in your group.

8 | TAKING SKILLS FURTHER

Outside of class, observe people speaking in public (giving a lecture or a speech). Notice how they stand, how they use eye contact, and how they speak. Try to think of some more strategies for giving presentations. Talk about your ideas in the next class.

 For additional listening practice on the topic of history, go to the *Open Forum* Web site (www.oup.com/elt/openforum) and follow the links.

Topics:	Math; computers
Listening Texts:	Radio program on the Fibonacci sequence; lecture on human computers
Listening Skill Focus:	Listening for examples
Speaking Skill Focus:	Giving opinions and responding to opinions
Vocabulary:	Adjectives with *–ing* and *–ed* endings
Pronunciation:	The *–ed* ending

1 | INTRODUCING THE TOPIC

1. Work with a partner. Make a list of the different ways that you use math and numbers in your everyday life.

2. Work in small groups and compare your lists.

2 | LISTENING PRACTICE

A Preparing to Listen

1. Work with a partner. Look at the sequence of numbers on the next page. See if you can figure out what the pattern is. What numbers come next in the sequence? Compare ideas with other students.

1, 1, 2, 3, 5, 8, 13, 21 ...

2. Look at the pictures and notice the number of petals on each flower. Do you see a pattern in the number of petals? How does the pattern relate to the sequence above?

B Listening for Main Ideas

You are going to listen to a radio program about the Fibonacci sequence. As you listen, number the topics in the order they are mentioned.

_____ Discovery of the Fibonacci sequence

_____ The sequence in art and music

_____ The sequence related to the human hand

_____ Numbers in the sequence

_____ The sequence in the natural world

C Focus on the Listening Skill: Listening for Examples

> **LISTENING SKILL**
>
> Speakers often give examples to clarify their point. The examples usually come after the point. Listening for the examples can help you understand the point that the speaker is making.

Listen to the program again. Write one example that is mentioned for each topic. Then compare answers with a partner.

Point	Example
1. The sequence in the natural world.	flowers,
2. The sequence in the human hand.	
3. The sequence in art.	
4. The sequence in music.	

D Listening for More Detail

Listen to the radio program again. As you listen, write *T* for true or *F* for false for each statement. Then compare answers with a partner. Listen again if necessary.

_____ 1. Each number in the Fibonacci sequence comes from the previous two numbers.

_____ 2. The sequence includes the number four.

_____ 3. The sequence ends when it gets to a very high number.

_____ 4. The numbers mentioned related to the human hand are all numbers in the sequence.

_____ 5. The sequence appears in Leonardo da Vinci's paintings in the form of spirals.

_____ 6. The sequence appears in art, but never in music.

_____ 7. A mathematician discovered the sequence in the early 1300s.

_____ 8. Fibonacci also introduced other mathematical ideas.

E Thinking and Speaking

Work in small groups. Discuss the questions.

1. How has the work of mathematicians changed since the time of Fibonacci?
2. Why do you think the Fibonacci sequence has fascinated mathematicians and scientists for more than 800 years?
3. How important do you think mathematics is for everyday life?

3 | VOCABULARY: Adjectives with –ing and –ed Endings

1. Many adjectives are formed by adding –ing or –ed to a verb. Read the sentences and the underlined adjectives. Which form (–ing or –ed) describes how the person feels? Which form describes what makes her feel this way?

   The Fibonacci sequence is <u>fascinating</u>. Emma wants to learn more about it.

   Emma is <u>fascinated</u> by the Fibonacci sequence. She wants to learn more about it.

2. Look at the adjectives below and check that you know what they mean. Use a dictionary if necessary.

   bored / boring   intrigued / intriguing

   confused / confusing   surprised / surprising

   exhausted / exhausting   tired / tiring

   interested / interesting

3. Circle the correct adjective forms to complete the paragraph.

   My friend Mindy is really (1) **interested / interesting** in mathematics. I think it's

   because she's very good at it. I'm not good at math, and usually I don't find it

   (2) **interested / interesting**. Most of the time math is (3) **confused / confusing** to

   me, and I'm (4) **bored / boring** by it. Mindy usually helps me with my math

   homework. Last week we studied the Fibonacci sequence at school, and for

   once, I was (5) **intrigued / intriguing** by something mathematical. In fact, it was

   (6) **fascinated / fascinating**. I stayed up until 3:00 a.m. reading about it. Of course,

   I was (7) **exhausted / exhausting** at school the next morning. Mindy was really

   (8) **surprised / surprising** when I told her why I was so (9) **tired / tiring**.

4. **Work in small groups. Discuss the questions.**

    1. What school subjects do you think are interesting or intriguing?

    2. Which subjects are sometimes confusing to you?

    3. What makes you feel tired or exhausted?

    4. When was the last time you were really surprised?

4 | LISTENING PRACTICE

A Preparing to Listen

1. **Work in small groups. Look at the photographs. Discuss the development of computers. How have computers changed? How have computers affected our lives?**

2. **Compare your ideas as a class.**

B Listening for Main Ideas

Listen to a lecture about human computers. Number the topics in the order they are mentioned.

    _____ Human computers in World War I and World War II

    _____ A book about human computers

    _____ A mathematical model of the orbit of Halley's comet

    _____ The kind of people who worked as human computers

    _____ Division of labor

C Listening for More Detail

🎧 Listen to the lecture again. Answer the questions. Then compare answers with a partner. Listen again if necessary.

1. What is the focus of the class that this lecture is from? _____

   _____

2. How many people worked together to calculate a model of Halley's comet? _____

   _____

3. How long did they work? _____

   _____

4. How did the French civil engineer manage to prepare 19 volumes of math tables?

   _____

   _____

5. How long did it take? _____

   _____

6. What kind of work did human computers do in World War I and World War II?

   _____

   _____

7. What type of people often worked as human computers? _____

   _____

8. Why did the author of the book about human computers become interested in the topic?

   _____

   _____

D Thinking and Speaking

Work with a partner. Discuss the questions. Then compare answers in small groups.

1. What roles do humans play in computing nowadays? How do you think this will change or not change over time?

2. How do you think computers might change in the future?

5 | PRONUNCIATION: The –ed Ending

FYI When pronouncing past tense verbs with *–ed* endings, add the extra syllable pronounced /id/ when the verb ends with a /t/ or /d/ sound (such as *want* or *divide*). With verbs that do not end in a /t/ or /d/ sound, the *–ed* ending does not add an extra syllable.

1. Listen to the sentences. In which three sentences is the *–ed* ending pronounced with an extra syllable?

    1. An engineer <u>wanted</u> to prepare 19 books.
    2. He <u>started</u> with a small group.
    3. They <u>worked</u> together.
    4. They <u>divided</u> the work.
    5. He <u>hired</u> 80 human computers.
    6. They <u>finished</u> the work after six years.

2. Practice saying the sentences above. Listen again to check your pronunciation.

3. Write sentences about yourself in the past tense. Use these verbs (or your own ideas). Then work with a partner and say your sentences.

    finished   needed   played   started   wanted   worked

6 | SPEAKING SKILLS: Giving Opinions and Responding to Opinions

SPEAKING SKILL

When you are having a discussion, use the expressions in the chart below to give your opinion and to respond to other people's opinions.

Giving an Opinion	Agreeing	Agreeing in Part	Disagreeing
I think . . . I don't think . . .	I agree.	Maybe, but . . . I see your point, but . . .	I don't agree. I'm not sure. / I'm not sure I agree.

1. Listen to the conversation. What are Monica and Toby discussing?

2. Listen again. Which expressions do the speakers use to give opinions and respond to opinions?

7 | SPEAKING PRACTICE

1. **Work with a partner. Look at the list of activities. What types of technology do you use for each of the activities?**

   Communicating with friends and family: _____

   Studying and doing research: _____

   Listening to music: _____

   Watching movies: _____

   Keeping track of your schedule and appointments: _____

   Taking photos: _____

   Playing games: _____

2. **Work in small groups. Compare your answers from above. Then discuss the questions below.**

   1. Compare technology in your life with technology when your parents were children. Think about the activities above and say how each one has changed because of technology.

   2. In your opinion, has technology made life simpler or more complicated?

   3. In your opinion, what has been the most important development in technology in the past 50 years? Give reasons for your answers.

   4. If you had to stop using two kinds of technology, which ones would be easiest for you to give up?

8 | TAKING SKILLS FURTHER

Listen to people giving opinions outside of class and pay attention to the expressions they use. Talk about what you noticed in the next class.

For additional listening practice on the topic of computers, go to the *Open Forum* Web site (www.oup.com/elt/openforum) and follow the links.

Topic:	Crime and the law
Listening Texts:	Interview about restorative justice; radio call-in program about legal questions
Listening Skill Focus:	Identifying important points
Speaking Skill Focus:	Rephrasing to check understanding
Vocabulary:	The adjective endings –al, –ent, –ive
Pronunciation:	Intonation with wh– questions

1 | INTRODUCING THE TOPIC

1. Look at the newspaper headlines. In which story has a person been found guilty?

1.

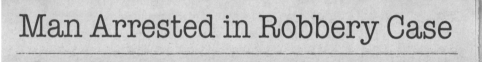

Man Arrested in Robbery Case

2.

Sixteen-Year-Old Offender Will Be Treated as an Adult

3.

Kidnappers Release Boy Unharmed

4.

Rock Star Is Victim of Purse Snatching

5.

Harrison Pleads Not Guilty on all Charges

6.

Woman Convicted in Museum Robbery

2. Find a word or expression in each headline to match the definitions below. Then compare answers with a partner.

1. Picked up by police and taken to a police station: _____*arrested*_____

2. A person who commits a crime: _____

3. Let someone go: _____

4. A person who has been injured or killed in a crime or accident: _____

5. States in court that he or she did not commit a crime: _____

6. Found guilty of a crime: _____

3. Work with a partner. Discuss the questions.

1. What crimes do you commonly read or hear about in the news?
2. How are these crimes usually punished?

2 | LISTENING PRACTICE

A Preparing to Listen

1. Work with a partner. Discuss the questions.

   1. Do you think prison is an effective form of punishment for crimes? Give reasons for your answer.

   2. What kinds of punishment are most effective? Why do you think so?

2. Work with another pair and compare your answers to the questions. Do you all agree?

B Listening for Main Ideas

 Listen to the interview about restorative justice. Then answer the question.

What are the two main aims of restorative justice? Mark the correct answers.

_____ To punish the offender

_____ To make the offender take responsibility for the crime

_____ To keep the offender out of prison

_____ To send the offender to prison

_____ To restore the victim of a crime

C Listening for More Detail

 Listen to the interview again. Write *T* for true or *F* for false for each statement. Then compare answers with a partner. Correct the false statements. Listen again if necessary.

_____ 1. According to the radio program, many people commit crimes again after they have spent time in prison.

_____ 2. Restorative justice focuses on punishing the offender.

_____ 3. In a typical restorative justice program, the offender must do something to make up for the damage that has been done.

_____ 4. According to Robert Sherman, some criminals do not feel responsibility for the damage they cause.

_____ 5. Victims often feel more afraid after they meet the offenders.

_____ 6. Restorative justice programs are particularly effective with young people.

_____ 7. Restorative justice is only used in the United States.

_____ 8. Restorative justice systems have been used by traditional societies.

D Focus on the Listening Skill: Identifying Important Points

LISTENING SKILL

When you are listening to formal talks or lectures, pay attention to expressions such as *in particular . . .* , *in fact . . .* , or *the main thing is. . . .* Speakers often use these expressions to emphasize an important or unusual point.

Listen to the extracts from the interview. After each extract, choose the answer that best completes the important point the speaker is making. Write down the expression the speaker uses to emphasize the point.

1. The speaker wants to emphasize the fact that restorative justice _____.
   a. is an old-fashioned way to deal with crime
   b. focuses on the effects of the crime on the community
   c. aims to help the offender take responsibility

   The speaker uses the expression: _____the main thing is_____

2. The speaker wants to emphasize the fact that _____.
   a. the boys cause a lot of damage
   b. the boys confess to the crime
   c. the boys meet the victims of the damage

   The speaker uses the expression: _____

3. The speaker wants to emphasize the fact that _____.
   a. the victims take part in the process
   b. meeting the offenders helps victims feel less afraid
   c. the victims have a chance to tell their side of the story

   The speaker uses the expression: _____

4. The speaker wants to emphasize the fact that _____.
   a. restorative justice is used all over the world
   b. there are different kinds of restorative justice programs
   c. restorative justice programs are sometimes based on traditional systems

   The speaker uses the expression: _____

E Thinking and Speaking

Work in pairs or small groups. Discuss the questions.

1. How might you use restorative justice to deal with the following criminals?

   • Someone who steals and crashes a car
   • A powerful businessperson who steals money from his or her own company
   • Someone who seriously injures another person during a robbery

2. Can you think of any cases where a restorative justice approach would not work well?

3 VOCABULARY: The Adjective Endings –al, –ent, –ive

1. Adjectives often end in –al, –ent, or –ive. Underline the adjective endings in this sentence. Then add the adjectives to the chart.

   Restorative justice is a different approach to the traditional court system.

–al	–ent	–ive
criminal	current	active
federal	innocent	alternative
legal	recent	effective
political	violent	positive
local	present	negative
_____	_____	_____

2. Read the following paragraph. Complete the paragraph using words from the chart. The first letter of each word is given.

   I like to watch the (1) _local_____ news every day because

   I want to know what is happening in my area. I also enjoy TV programs

   about (2) _c_____ events. I enjoy reading about politics

   and watching shows about (3) _p_____ issues.

3. The following paragraph summarizes the radio report about restorative justice. Complete the paragraph using words from the chart. The first letter of each word is given.

Restorative justice is an (4) a_____

approach to dealing with crime, and it is particularly

(5) e_____ with young offenders. Research

indicates that restorative justice programs have

a (6) p_____ effect. These programs are

gradually being introduced to the (7) c_____

justice system and are used even for (8) v_____

crimes such as murder.

4. Read this advertisement for a lawyer's office. Complete the advertisement using words from the chart.

JACKSON AND ROBERTS LAW FIRM
Did you know that credit card fraud is a (9) f_____
offence? If you have been a victim of credit card fraud, contact our
lawyers for free (10) l_____ advice.
Dial 1.800.LAW HELP

5. Work with a partner. Think of a recent news story about a crime or about politics. Tell your partner about the news story.

4 LISTENING PRACTICE

A Preparing to Listen

Work with a partner. Discuss the legal questions below.

1. If you find something valuable on the street, can you legally keep it? Can you sell it and keep the money? What should you do?

2. If a visitor is injured in your home, are you legally responsible for the injury? Do you have to pay for the victim's medical costs? Does it matter whether you own the home or rent it?

B Listening for Main Ideas

Listen to the radio show. Answer the questions.

1. What advice does the lawyer give in the first situation?
   a. The woman must return the painting to the owners.
   b. The woman should return the painting to the owners.

2. What does the lawyer say about the second situation?
   a. The tenant is not liable (legally responsible for damage) in this situation.
   b. The tenant could be liable in this situation.

C Listening for More Detail

Listen to the radio program again. As you listen, choose the correct answer to complete each statement. Compare your answers with a partner. Listen again if necessary.

1. Patty found a painting _____.
   a. in her neighbor's yard
   b. in front of her home
   c. in front of her neighbor's home

2. After she took it home, she discovered that the painting was _____.
   a. signed
   b. stolen
   c. valuable

3. She can legally keep the painting because _____.
   a. her neighbors threw it away
   b. she found it
   c. she found that it was valuable

4. The lawyer thinks that she should return the painting because _____.
   a. her neighbors want it back
   b. her neighbors didn't know it was valuable
   c. her neighbors could hold her responsible

5. The danger in Andrew's house is _____.
   a. a hole in the floor
   b. a hole in the stairs
   c. on the second floor

6. Andrew is worried because _____.
   a. he might get hurt
   b. he can't afford to repair it
   c. someone might get hurt and hold him responsible

7. Andrew has _____ about the situation.
   a. told the landlord
   b. not told the landlord
   c. written to the landlord

8. In this situation, _____ could be liable.
   a. Andrew
   b. the landlord
   c. both Andrew and the landlord

D Working Out Unknown Vocabulary

Listen to the extracts from the radio program. Listen for the words and expressions in italics. Choose the correct meaning for each one. Compare answers with a partner.

1. The *curb* is probably _____.
   a. the edge of the sidewalk near the street
   b. the middle of the street

2. *Ethically* probably means _____.
   a. according to the law
   b. morally, in terms of right and wrong

3. *Legally obligated* probably means _____.
   a. expected to do something
   b. required to do something by law

4. *Notify* probably means _____.
   a. inform someone of something
   b. visit someone

E Thinking and Speaking

Work in pairs or small groups. Discuss the questions.

1. In the first situation, do you agree with the lawyer's advice to return the painting? Would you follow that advice?

2. Think of another situation like the second case where a renter could be held responsible for an injury or for damage. Why is it important for a tenant to notify a landlord in writing?

5 | PRONUNCIATION: Intonation with *Wh–* Questions

FYI *Wh–* questions (questions that use *who, what, when, where, why,* or *how*) are usually spoken with falling intonation, like statements. This can make it difficult to recognize questions, because the intonation is the same as for regular statements.

🎧 1. Listen to the questions from the radio program. Repeat the questions, paying attention to the intonation.

🎧 2. Listen to the questions about the radio program. Write the questions.

1. _____

2. _____

3. _____

4. _____

5. _____

3. Ask and answer the questions in pairs. Use falling intonation when asking the questions.

6 | SPEAKING SKILLS: Rephrasing to Check Understanding

◦ SPEAKING SKILL

Rephrasing is one way to check that you have understood what a speaker has said. Use the expressions in the box to rephrase what someone else says.

> Oh, you mean . . .
> You're saying / You said that . . .
> So you think . . .
> So you want to know . . .

🎧 1. Listen to an extract from the radio program. What rephrasing expressions do you hear?

7 | SPEAKING PRACTICE

1. Work in small groups. Discuss each situation. Try to answer the question that is asked in each situation.

> 1. "I bought a used car from my neighbor. When I took it on a test-drive, it ran fine, so I paid him $2,000 for the car. However, since bringing it home, I've had several problems. Now, the car won't even start! I just want to return the car and get my money back. What rights do I have?"

> 2. "My friend and I signed a one-year agreement for our apartment. We each paid half the rent for six months. Now she has left to move in with another friend, and the landlord is asking me to pay the whole rent by myself. Can the landlord do this?"

> 3. "I was riding my bike past a neighbor's house when their dog ran out and tried to bite my leg. I fell off the bike and injured my right arm. I couldn't go to work for two weeks. The dog's owner said his dog had never done that before. Is the dog's owner liable for the money I lost?"

2. Now read the legal information about each situation. After reading the legal information, what advice would you give each person?

   1. According to United States law, if you buy a used car from an automobile dealer, the dealer usually has to honor whatever warranty he or she gave. But if you buy a car from a private owner, you are taking a chance. In this case, the seller is not legally required to give you your money back or even to repair the car.

   2. According to United States law, since you signed the lease, you are responsible to pay the full month's rent if the other person does not pay.

   3. According to United States law, the dog owner is often not liable if this is the first time the dog has ever attacked anyone. However, many states are taking a stricter approach, so you could win a case even if this is the first time the dog has behaved this way. Of course, you have a better chance of winning the case if you can prove that the dog has attacked people before.

8 | TAKING SKILLS FURTHER

The next time you have difficulty understanding what someone is saying, try to rephrase what the person has said using one or more of the rephrasing expressions. Talk about your experiences in the next class.

For additional listening practice on the topic of crime and the law, go to the *Open Forum* Web site (www.oup.com/elt/openforum) and follow the links.